IMAGES
of America

LIGHTHOUSES OF
EASTERN MICHIGAN

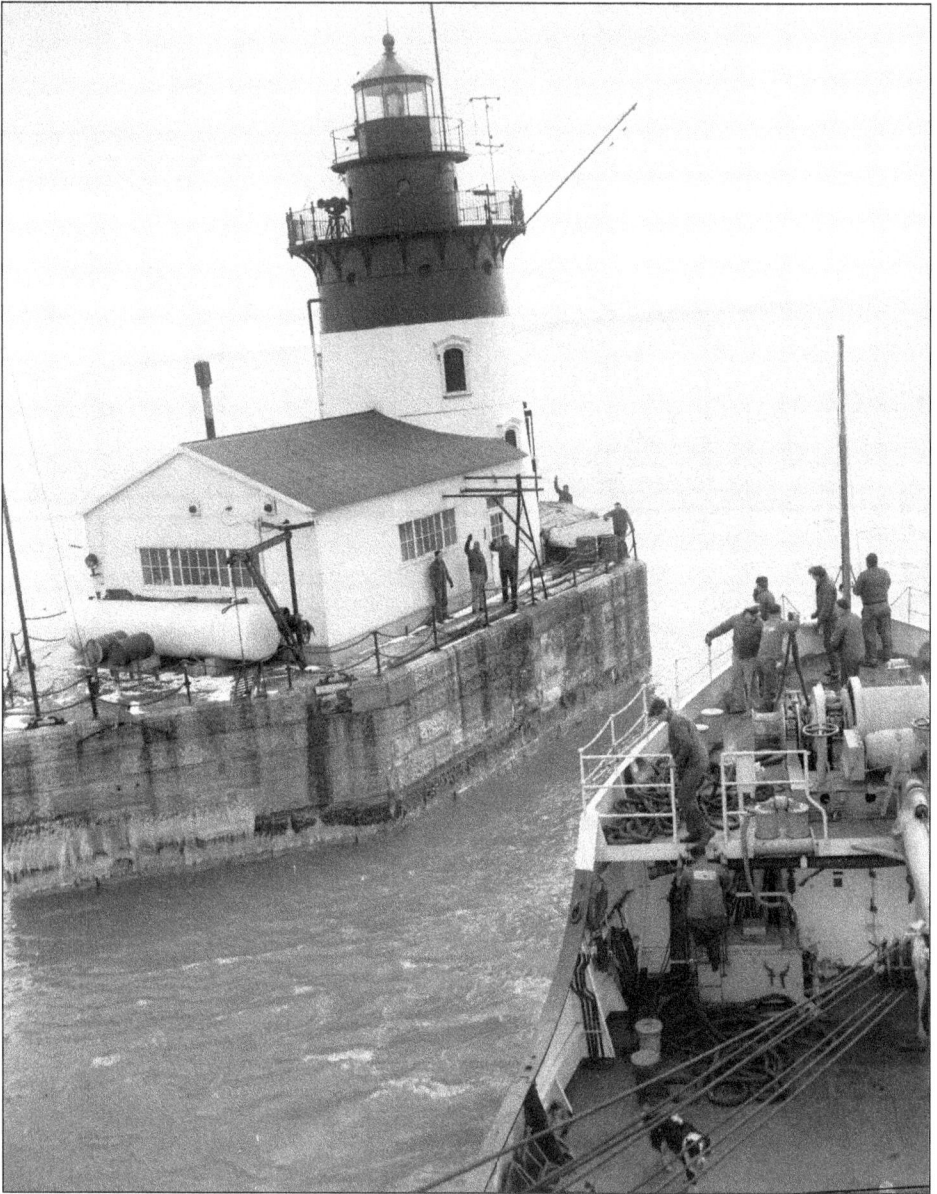

Buoy and lighthouse tender *Acacia* approaches the 1885 Detroit River Lighthouse in 1950. The 634-foot freighter *Buffalo* hit the Detroit River Lighthouse on December 12, 1997. The bow of the steel-hulled ship collapsed, stamped with the imprint of the lighthouse crib like a car part in an auto-stamping plant. The ship sustained $1.2 million in damage, while the crib had very minor damage. The elongated, hexagon crib was built with two points at each end to facilitate the movement of ice, water—and sometimes freighters. (Walter P. Reuther Library, Wayne State University.)

ON THE COVER: Round Island Lighthouse, pictured between 1895 and 1910, guided ships into the Mackinac Island Harbor. This light symbolizes everything that is good about Michigan's 100-plus lighthouses and their restoration by the concerned people of Michigan and the Great Lakes Lighthouse Keepers Association. (Mackinac State Historic Parks Collection.)

IMAGES
of America

LIGHTHOUSES OF
EASTERN MICHIGAN

Wil and Pat O'Connell

ARCADIA
PUBLISHING

Dedicated to Dick and Ida Lower and Joseph and Mary O'Connell.

In this rare 1913 photograph, a large steam freighter passes the Fort Gratiot Lighthouse as people watch from the beach. Notice the masts; even the builders were not confident in their steam engines and wanted a backup plan. A Port Huron Museum brochure reads: "Historic Fort Gratiot Lighthouse is one of the most recognizable and beloved landmarks on the Great Lakes. It is an object of pride for locals, a must see for visitors and an important landmark for sailors." (Port Huron Museum.)

CONTENTS

Acknowledgments   6

Introduction   7

1.   The Soo Locks and The Straits Lighthouses   9

2.   A Toppled Tower and Upper Lake Huron Lighthouses   29

3.   Spectacle, DeTour, and the Beloved Forty Mile Lighthouses   37

4.   A Mystery among Alpena Area Lighthouses   45

5.   A Burning Ship Rescue and Mid-Michigan Lighthouses   53

6.   Lighthouses during the "White Hurricane"   61

7.   An Unhappy Keeper and St. Clair Lighthouses   71

8.   Secrets of Slightly Sinful Lighthouses   85

9.   Lost Lighthouses of the Detroit River   107

10.   Ships that Seldom Sail   121

Lighthouse Museums and Organizations   126

Bibliography   127

ACKNOWLEDGMENTS

This book would not be possible without the help of Jim and Nancy Reid (JNR) of Galion, Ohio. Their generous hospitality, encouragement, good company, and fun-filled conversations, as well as Jim's computer expertise and Nancy's gourmet meals, greatly inspired us and made tedious computer work a pleasure. Thanks to Elizabeth Clemens, audiovisual archivist at the Walter P. Reuther Library, at Wayne State University, for the rare photographs of slightly sinful lighthouses and information on the secret activities occurring around these lights; Terry Pepper, executive director of Great Lakes Lighthouse Keepers Association for his vast knowledge of Great Lakes lighthouses; Izzy Donnelly, curator at the Grosse Pointe Historical Society (GPHS); Robert Graham, archivist at the Bowling Green State University (BGSU) for numerous, interesting newspaper articles on the November 1913 storm; Katherine Bancroft, director of education and collections, and Doug Bancroft, director of exhibits, at the Port Huron Museum (PHM); Bryon Jaeschke, registrar of the Mackinac State Historic Parks Collection; Clare Koester at the Grosse Ile Historical Society; Julie Meyerle, archivist at the Michigan State Archives (MSA); Sandy Shalton, acquisitions editor at Arcadia Publishing; Christopher Gillcrist of the Great Lakes Historical Society (GLHS), renamed National Great Lakes Museum in Toledo, Ohio; Sarah Clifford of Mansfield, Ohio; the United States Coast Guard (USCG); and Mary Ilario, still photograph reference team, National Archives and Records Administration (NARA). Photographs from the author's collection are marked AC.

Wil and Pat O'Connell are also authors of Images of America: *Ohio Lighthouses* for Arcadia Publishing.

INTRODUCTION

Lighthouses and lightships were designed to save lives and vessels. This is a statement that reflects the power of the Great Lakes, as Michigan has more lighthouses than any other state in the country. Interspersed along the journey this book takes from the Straits of Mackinac and the Soo Locks, down Lake Huron, and into Lake St. Clair and the Detroit River are some harrowing experiences captains and sailors had traveling these waterways. They are stories of the struggle to save ships and crew members. The unleashed power of the Great Lakes, such as the force of a November storm in 1913 given the name "White Hurricane," tested the value of using lighthouse beacons as a guide. The significance of these structures proved to be priceless to the men sailing the waters of eastern Michigan.

Lighthouses were of importance to politicians and businessmen as well, who wanted to increase commerce and bring prosperity to Michigan cities and the state. As trade increased along Great Lakes waterways, ship owners and insurance companies interested in tamping down the amount of shipwrecks also became heavily involved with the development of lighthouses.

This uptick in trade occurred in the 1800s, when the lumber and fishing industries in Michigan were becoming more viable. After iron ore was discovered in the mid-1850s in the upper Great Lakes and the first incarnation of the Soo Locks opened in 1855, ships slowly began to transport more iron ore to Detroit and other hubs. Enough was shipped to help make the steel that eventually became the backbone of the country's infrastructure as well as later launch the auto industry. By the turn of the century, Michigan had become the land of opportunity; fortunes were made in the automotive, shipping, and steel industries. People migrated to the state to capitalize on the wealth of industrial work found in cities such as Detroit, Lansing, Flint, and Cadillac. As shipping increased, so did the need for lighthouses—they played a major role in the economic growth of Michigan.

Rare images, some 100 to 150 years old and never seen before, depict these Michigan lighthouses, their keepers, and a lifestyle different from today's reality. It was a simpler era, but one that could be extremely perilous given the situation. A good example is the Spectacle Reef Lighthouse, so isolated and dangerous that only bachelors, with their dogs, were allowed to serve as keepers. Blizzards and "November gales" constantly buffeted this lighthouse—among many in eastern Michigan—and tested a keeper's confidence in the man-made structure built in 1874.

During Prohibition, using lighthouse beacons to guide them, ordinary citizens made fortunes transporting booze from Canada to Detroit in boats, mostly at night. It was a cat-and-mouse game on both sides of the law throughout the region, with Detroit-area lighthouses bearing witness to more than their fair share of the era's stories, documented in chapter eight, "Secrets of Slightly Sinful Lighthouses."

It is impossible to revisit all of the fascinating stories about the stalwart, brave people who developed eastern Michigan into an economic engine via Lake Huron and its tributaries—who plied its fickle waters, manned its lonely lighthouses, and sailed its risky lightships—but this book was written to salute all of them and their courage.

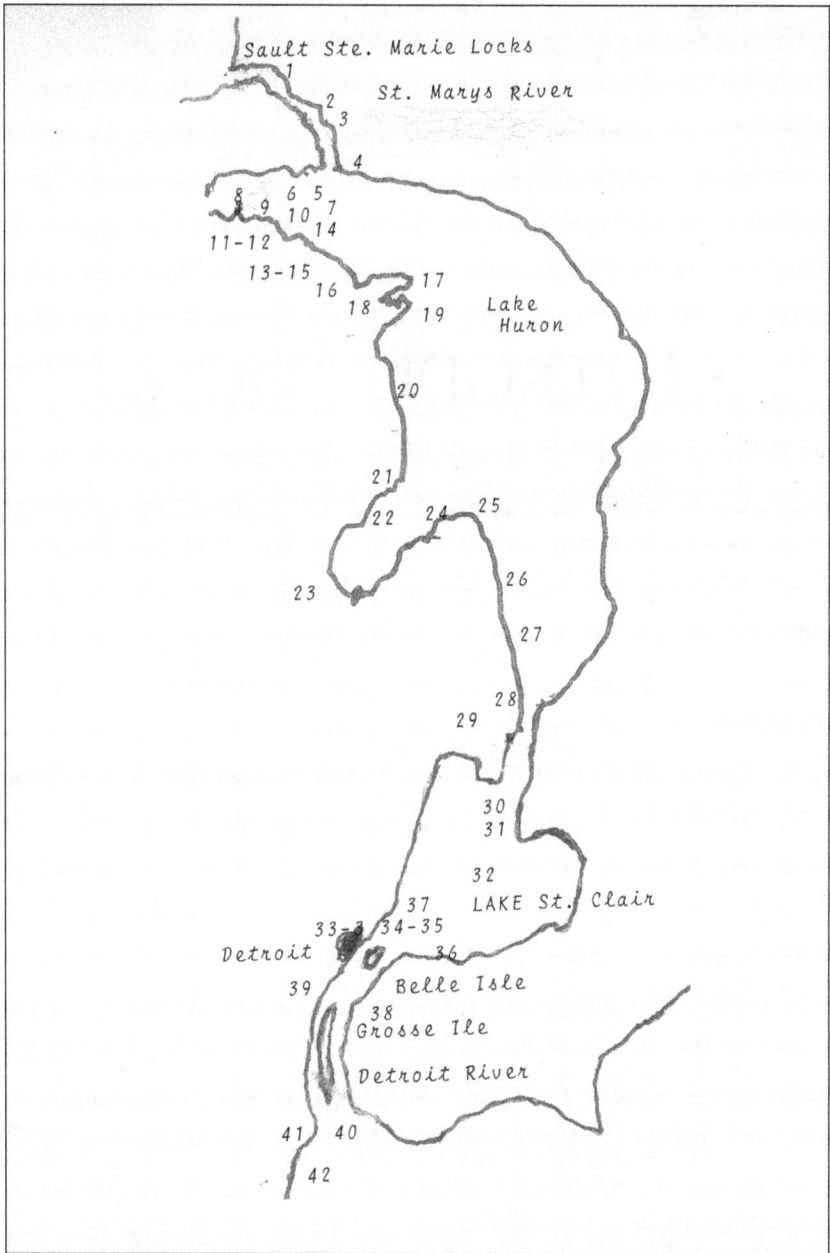

Lighthouses: 1. Little Rapids Cut; 2. Round Island (St. Mary's River); 3. Pipe Island; 4. Frying Pan Island; 5. DeTour Reef; 6. Martin Reef; 7. Spectacle Reef; 8. Round Island (Straits of Mackinac); 9. Round Island Passage; 10. Bois Blanc; 11. Cheboygan Main; 12. Cheboygan Crib; 13. Fourteen Foot Shoal; 14. Poe Reef; 15. Forty Mile Point; 16. Old and New Presque Isle; 17. Middle Island; 18. Alpena; 19. Thunder Bay Island; 20. Sturgeon Point; 21. Tawas Point; 22. Gravelly Shoal; 23. Saginaw Bay; 24. Port Austin Reef; 25. Pointe aux Barques; 26. Harbor Beach; 27. Port Sanilac; 28. Fort Gratiot; 29. Port Huron Lightship; 30. St. Clair Range and Ship Canal; 31. Harsens Island; 32. Lake St. Clair; 33. Belle Isle; 34. Livingston Memorial; 35. Mama Juda; 36. Peche Island Rear Range; 37. Windmill Point; 38. Grosse Ile North and South Channel and Front and Rear Range; 39. Grassy Island North and South Channel; 40. Detroit River; 41. Gibraltar; and 42. Monroe. (AC.)

One

THE SOO LOCKS AND THE STRAITS LIGHTHOUSES

On June 9, 1909, the *Crescent City*, loaded with ore and down bound from Marquette on Lake Superior to Lake Huron and past the Round Island Light, pulled behind the steamer *Assinibola*, with 300 passengers, so both ships could go through the Sault Ste. Marie locks together.

But something went wrong. The *Perry G. Walker*, below the lock and up bound, suddenly tore away from the pier, ramming and tearing one of the lower lock gates from its hinges. In an interview with a *Cleveland Plains Dealer* journalist, Capt. Frank Rice of the *Crescent City* explained:

> Instantly, 300 miles of pent-up Lake Superior water came rushing through the lock, turning it into a seething rapids, at the end of which was a 20 foot cataract [drop] where the lock gate had been. The first I knew of disaster was when the stern of the *Assinibola* in front of us reared out of the water, her nose down for the fateful plunge. We were being swept down toward her at a speed of 30 miles per hour, so that everything happened in a space of seconds. Closer and closer we came to the *Assinibola*. Then with a deafening crash, over the *Assinibola* went. Nearer and nearer the *Crescent City* bore down toward that same cataract, like a chip of wood on the bosom of the Niagara, a plaything of the Gods, and I and all of us, powerless to lift a finger to save either life or ship. Down went our bow, down, down, down, and every movable object on deck came tumbling forward. For a brief second we seemed to hang there on the edge of the cataract, suspended in midair. Then we heard the crunching of the hull across the top of the lock and the ship seemed to be crumbling like an eggshell in the hand of a giant. I was clinging to every support, and I closed my eyes as we went over. "This is the end," I thought. "Goodbye Old World."

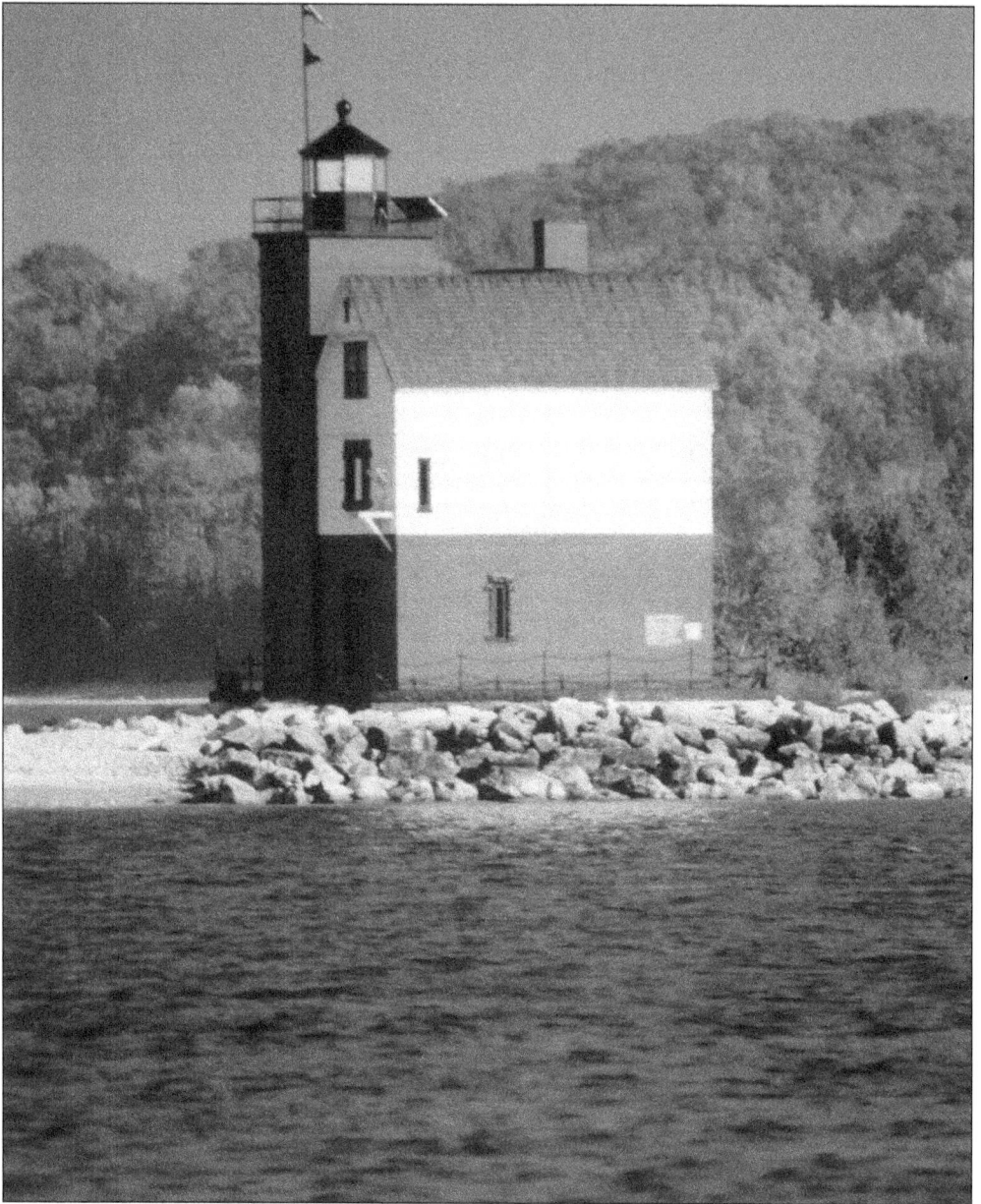

Captain Rice of the *Crescent City* continued, "But we floated! The *Assinibola* lay directly in our path as we swept on. But we could clear her, for she, too, was borne along on the irresistible flood of moving water. And then the sailors on the *Assinibola* let go her anchors! The ship stopped dead before us! The *Perry G. Walker* lay to port. Could we, in the brief space of seconds and moving forward with the rapid current, find our way between the *Assinibola*, tugging at her anchors, and the *Perry G. Walker*? I signaled full speed astern. The old ship responded, and though she swept on, her stern veered around to starboard a second before it seemed inevitable that we should strike the *Assinibola* amidships, sending her and her 300 passengers to the bottom. Now I prayed and hoped. We struck the *Assinibola*, but it was a glancing blow, and then we glided through the narrow space between the two steamers. . . . We just went through (Hades), that's all." The Round Island Lighthouse is pictured in 2000. (AC.)

Soo, Mich. Locking through at night.

"My father was C.C. Allen, a captain," Captain Allen told a journalist for a *Cleveland Plain Dealer* article in 1924. "There were nine children; I'm the oldest. I got my pilot's license at 21 only because they couldn't legally give it to me any sooner. I was 16 when I shipped with the *Charles J. Sheffield* for the last time. It was Friday, June 13, 1889. I'm not superstitious [but] no ship would sail on Friday in the old days. She might be ready to sail, but she'd never hoist anchor. Well, this was the 13th of the month and a Friday, 5:00 p.m. [when we left for the Soo Locks]." The Soo Locks are pictured about 1915. (AC.)

"I had held the watch the night before and was sleeping in my bunk between decks," continued Captain Allen. "We were steaming through a heavy fog 50 miles north of the Soo Locks. Suddenly there was a grinding crash, and I found myself on the floor. If I had any thought at all it was that we had gone upon the rocks. I grabbed my pants and started for the stairs. Everything between decks was all awry. The stairs normally sloped up at an angle of about 75 degrees; but now they stood straight up. The door was tilted forward, and clothing and loose articles rolled crazily down." The Soo Locks are pictured in 1920. (AC.)

"Once on deck I saw the huge bulk of the steamer, *North Star*, looming up hazily over us through the fog," Captain Allen stated. "She had rammed us (*Charles J. Sheffield*), just forward of the boiler house on the port side, and a great, gaping wound yawned in her bow big enough to drive a street car through. A ladder was dropped over the side of the *North Star* and I saw my father scramble up. As he reached the deck, the *Sheffield* suddenly settled and the ladder toppled into the sea. An instant of delay would have plunged him overboard to his death." The Soo Locks are pictured here—one with a plane—around 1920. (AC.)

"The ship was sinking fast and we were going down with it. I thought we were gone," Captain Allen described. "A coiled rope, like a great snake, came hurtling toward us. We seized and made it fast. Over that rope I climbed aboard the *North Star*. And every one of the crew of 18 was saved. Four minutes later we saw the masts of the *Sheffield* settle beneath the waves. And so, with everything lost save life itself, the *North Star* went limping with us into Sault Ste. Marie." Lake, rail, and motor transportation are pictured above in 1922 at Union Depot, used jointly by Canadian Pacific, Duluth, South Shore and Atlantic, and Soo Line railroads. *Bide-a-Wee* enters the Soo Locks in the photograph below. (AC.)

Excursion Yacht "Bide-a-Wee"

Entering Lock, Sault Ste. Marie, Mich.

Forcing a Channel Through The Ice, St. Mary's River, Soo, Mich

The smoke-producing steam engine freighters seen here break ice in the St. Mary's River near the Soo Locks during the spring in the 1900s. (AD.)

The 1895 Round Island Lighthouse has always been a guiding beacon for passenger ships steaming into the harbor at Mackinac Island, a booming resort area for wealthy tourists. It became famous when it was featured in the film *Somewhere in Time*. Its survival had been a constant battle for people in Michigan who love the lighthouse. (Mackinac State Historic Parks Collection.)

After it was automated in 1924 and deactivated in 1947, US Coast Guard personnel suggested in 1955 that the lighthouse should be destroyed. Fate intervened, and the lighthouse was classified as "surplus." Three years later, Round Island and its lighthouse were transferred to the US Forest Service and classified a National Scenic Area. The lighthouse, pictured here in 2008, was saved. (AC.)

In 1972, a severe storm washed away the southwest corner of the Round Island Lighthouse, and it was poised to collapse. Residents formed the Friends of the Round Island Lighthouse and raised money to repair the damage. In 1974, the Mackinac Island Historical Society and Hiawatha National Forest signed an agreement to restore the lighthouse. (Mackinac State Historic Parks Collection.)

In April 1974, the US Forest Service gave notice that the Round Island Lighthouse had to be razed for safety reasons. In response, residents sent in paperwork for it to be preserved as a historic site. In August 1974, the lighthouse was added to the National Register of Historic Places, and its future again seemed secure. Then, the US Forest Service said there was no funding available for its restoration; in 1975, Pres. Gerald Ford vetoed $125,000 appropriated to save the lighthouse. Again, the Friends of Round Island Lighthouse came through with funds necessary, in November 1975, to repair a hole in the wall and save the lighthouse. (AC.)

When high water in 1986 damaged the outhouse and Round Island Lighthouse, more costly repairs were needed, and people again saved the light. In 1995, the Great Lakes Lighthouse Keepers Association and Boy Scout Troop No. 323 of Freeland, Michigan, joined in the fight to save and restore the Round Island Lighthouse, pictured here restored. Today, passing the lighthouse to Mackinac Island, the bright red and white lighthouse brings back fond memories for the people who fought to preserve it. (AC.)

The white 1948 Round Island Passage Light near Mackinac Island is a 60-foot concrete tower on a concrete pier over a wooden crib. With a foghorn and radio beacon, its 1973 automated, 190-millimeter optic lens guides mariners through the passage to the harbor at Mackinac Island. (AC.)

A humorous c. 2009 photograph, taken on a dock at Mackinac Island, shows a man carrying his dog in a backpack and gives new meaning to the phrase, "Walking the dog." (AC.)

People love visiting Mackinac Island. As the steamer docks welcome visitors in the early 1900s, the watchful eyes of Fort Mackinac, built in 1780 on a grassy hill 133 feet above the lake, guards the deepwater harbor and the Straits of Mackinac. The British commandeered the island from the French in 1761. (AC.)

Horse-drawn carriages take affluent people up and down Main Street in July 1910. Like a rare gem, Mackinac Island is unique—the pride of Michigan. Dignitaries, politicians, and presidents have visited the island through the years. (AC.)

Main Street, Mackinac Island, Mich.

Above, bicycles, horses, and carriages mingle harmoniously on the main street of Mackinac Island in 1927. A peaceful place to get away from it all, people love visiting the island to enjoy its idyllic beauty. Below, a vintage, 38-foot wooden cruiser passes the island's world-famous 1887 Grand Hotel. (AC.)

The cruise ship SS *North West* unloads passengers at Arnold Dock on Mackinac Island. The luxurious 500-plus-passenger ship, built in 1895, and her sister ship *Northland* carried people from Buffalo, New York, to Duluth, Minnesota. In 1913, east and west breakwaters were built to protect the harbor. (AC.)

The *City of Mackinac*, a Detroit and Cleveland Navigation Co. ship running between Detroit and Mackinac Island, is pictured in the background while the *South American* cruise ship takes on passengers at a Mackinac Island dock about 1920. (AC.)

A man with goggles, opening up the engine in his speedboat, appears to be famous speedboat driver and builder Gar Wood. A speedboat like the one pictured, *Miss America I*, won the 1921 Harnsworth trophy with Wood at the helm. The two giants in wood boat building on the St. Clair River were Gar Wood and Chris Smith of Chris-Craft at Algonac, Michigan. Demand for premium speedboats peaked during Prohibition, when both sides of the struggle bought the fastest speedboats these two builders could produce. In the background, the 1887 Grand Hotel invites people who demand the best in everything. It is *the* place to stay for the affluent of society. With nearly 400 rooms, it is one of the largest summer resorts in the world. The 1887 New Mackinac Hotel, pictured below in 1927, was demolished in 1939, while the 1920 New Murray Hotel, to the right of the New Mackinac, is still operating. (AC.)

West of Round Island Lighthouse, the famous 1957 Mackinac Bridge invites adventurers to the Upper Peninsula. Although millions of cars have crossed the Mackinac Bridge safely, people like to talk about the day the wind blew a compact car off the bridge; this is a bit of American apocrypha. In reality, it was a Friday evening, September 22, 1989, and the driver, 31-year-old Leslie Ann Pluhar, was excited about meeting her boyfriend for the weekend. After passing a truck, she lost control of her small, 1987 Yugo, and it swerved left of center onto the median strip. (JNR.)

On the bridge, the wind speed was 35 miles per hour and Leslie's speed was 55 to 63 miles per hour. She then swerved right, off the median strip but for some reason kept turning right toward the side of the bridge until she was headed straight for the guardrail. When she hit it, the forward momentum raised the car up, and it flipped over the railing. The car hit various parts of the bridge before plunging 170 feet to the water below. One witness described the car as being like a feather floating in the air when it flew from the bridge and fell into the lake. Another witness wondered why her brake lights did not come on. (JNR.)

U. S. LIGHT HOUSE AND FOG SIGNAL,
MACKINAW CITY, MICH.

Old Mackinac Point Lighthouse, built like a castle in 1892, guided ships through the Straits of Mackinac and car ferries crossing to St. Ignace. In 1957, its light became obsolete with the completion of the Mackinac Bridge. In 1960, the Mackinac State Historic Parks acquired and restored the lighthouse. Visitors are welcome summer through fall. (AC.)

The 57-foot, octagonal Vidal Shoals Rear Range Light, pictured in the early 1900s near the International Train Bridge, guided ships into the Soo Locks. This light and a shorter front range light were replaced by lighted buoys. (AC.)

Ships bound from the Sault Ste. Marie Locks navigated the narrow St. Mary's River and passed Little Rapids Cut Light, Round Island Light, Pipe Island Light, and Frying Pan Island Light. The keeper lived on shore, while the assistant keeper and his family lived in the 1895 Little Rapids Cut Lighthouse, pictured on a crib six feet above the water. Both keepers tended range lights in the area. In 1911, this light was automated, and it was eventually razed in 1929. (NARA.)

The 1892 Round Island Lighthouse in lower St. Mary's River was doused in 1923 when a skeletal tower was erected with an automated light. In 1999, a Charlevoix couple bought the island and refurbished lighthouse. (NARA.)

27

Established on May 12, 1888, the Pipe Island Lighthouse Fifth Order Fresnel lens displayed a fixed red light from a 33-foot tower until 1937, when a skeletal tower with an automated light replaced it. Today, John and Mary Kostecki of Cedarville own the island and restored lighthouse, offering it as a vacation rental. (USCG.)

Displaying its light for the first time on October 1, 1882, Frying Pan Island Lighthouse was built two miles above the mouth of St. Mary's River. Two lights were later built on Pipe Island two miles to the north and also in the river. In 1894, the light was painted white, and in 1903 a two-story keeper's house was added. The light was discontinued in 1956 and replaced by an automatic light on a pole. (USCG.)

Two

A Toppled Tower and Upper Lake Huron Lighthouses

On December 9, 1837, Ever Ward, the first Bois Blanc Island Lighthouse keeper, was visiting Mackinac Island. His daughter Emily and her younger brother were tending the light when a terrible storm blew in from the east. Realizing the conical lighthouse might collapse, Emily made five trips up and down the tower to remove 13 Winslow Lewis lamps, reflectors, and other valuable items. Only minutes after retreating to the safety of the house, Emily and her brother watched the tower topple into a heap.

Like the gold-mining towns that sprung up overnight in the West, Duncan City and Cheboygan were boomtowns because of lumber. Cheboygan Crib Light, Cheboygan Main Light, and Range Light were built to aid in shipping lumber. By 1890, there were eight lumber mills in the area, with Duncan Mill the largest. When the religious Thompson Smith bought Duncan Mill, he outlawed bars in Duncan City. Apparently, hardworking lumberjacks liked their whiskey, as nearby Cheboygan had over 40 salons in 1895. A horrendous fire swept through Duncan Lumber Mill in 1898, destroying Duncan City—and Cheboygan and its bars survived.

People protested when the US Coast Guard announced they would destroy the 1884 Cheboygan Crib Light. The Coast Guard relented, donating the light to City of Cheboygan. In 1984, the tower was moved to Gordon Turner Park. Members of the Great Lakes Lighthouse Keepers Association and area residents restored the light for all to enjoy.

The second Bois Blanc Island Lighthouse, pictured here in 1904, was built in 1838 on higher ground, 150 feet behind the first light. A Fourth Order Fresnel lens was installed in 1857 and was moved to third lighthouse in 1867. The light was extinguished in 1924. (NARA.)

On August 24, 1925, Earl Coffey bought Bois Blanc Island Light for $1,000. Today, two Chicago-area families, Martin and Reinhart Jahn, industrialists, own the lighthouse and have restored it. (Walter P. Reuther Library, Wayne State University.)

The brown, cast-iron Cheboygan Crib Light, put into operation in 1884, was painted white in 1901. A fog bell was added in 1911, and the light was automated in 1929. (USCG.)

Members of the Great Lakes Lighthouse Keepers Association and area residents restored the Cheboygan Crib Light, pictured here, and moved it to Gordon Turner Park in 1984. (AC.)

The first 1851 Cheboygan Main Lighthouse, rebuilt in the 1860s and again in the 1870s, is pictured on October 22, 1913. It was abandoned and torn down in the 1930s. (USCG.)

The Cheboygan River Front Range Light at the mouth of the Cheboygan River, pictured here in 1904, was first lit on September 30, 1880. The wooden Rear Range Tower was replaced by a 75-foot skeletal tower in 1900. Both lights were automated in 1928. Members of the Great Lakes Lighthouse Keepers Association have donated time and money to restore the Cheboygan Front River Range Light, and today it casts a light beneficial to boaters entering the Cheboygan River. (USCG.)

The Cheboygan River Front Range Light was active until 1982. It was purchased in 2004 and restored to its former glory (pictured) by the Great Lakes Lighthouse Keepers Association. (AC.)

The attractive, shuttered Fourteen Foot Shoal Lighthouse was put into operation in 1930. It looks like a cute house, but no one lived here; it only housed equipment. The light and foghorn were remotely controlled by the keepers at the Poe Reef Lighthouse a few miles away. This light replaced the Cheboygan Crib Light. (USCG.)

At the beginning of the season, the first keepers at the 1927 Martin Reef Lighthouse (pictured here) had to chip through ice to open the door so they could start the oil furnace. The Art Deco–style tower was made of reinforced concrete over steel and was built to last. This lighthouse replaced Martin Reef Lightship in 1927. The first level held machinery that operated the station's equipment; the second floor had an office, bathroom, and kitchen; and the third floor housed bedrooms. A watch room at the top of the structure supported a cast-iron lantern with a Fourth Order Fresnel lens. In 1939, electric generators were installed. The light station was transferred to the Bureau of Indian Affairs in 2000. (USCG.)

A courageous man sits on a swing made of rope and dangles between a floating derrick and Martin Reef Pier during construction. It was dangerous work. Notice that he is not wearing a life preserver. (NARA.)

The unusual calm and stillness of a peaceful Lake Huron sends the heart soaring and stirs the soul. Its clear blue water invites the adventurous, the curious, and those who enjoy being and working on a boat on the water. In the wonderment of this foggy morning, men are placing the Martin Reef crib into position on July 24, 1925. (NARA.)

With the completion of the Martin Reef Lighthouse in 1927, the experienced workers began building an identical lighthouse at Poe Reef, pictured here, which replaced the Poe Reef Lightship in 1929. As on the previous page, notice the man hanging onto side of the pier without a protective helmet or life preserver. The bottom of the lighthouse was eventually painted black to distinguish it from Martin Reef Lighthouse. The light was automated in 1974. (USCG.)

Appearing to have a "halo" over it, the Poe Reef Lighthouse, pictured in May 1929, is seen partially complete. (NARA.)

The 1929 Poe Reef Lighthouse is pictured below with the keeper and a small boat in front of the impressive tower. (USCG.)

Three

SPECTACLE, DETOUR, AND THE BELOVED FORTY MILE LIGHTHOUSES

On October 19, 1902, the captain and crew of the steamboat *Joseph F. Fay* heard loud noises of wood splintering from the rear of the ship as it was being pulled apart. Their steamboat was towing a large barge, and the force from the waves on the taut towline began pulling the back end from the ship. The crew, their eyes wide with disbelief, watched the ship's stern fall into the lake and disappear. It has to be one of the strangest events that ever happened on Lake Huron.

Having only three-quarters of a ship left and water pouring in, the captain turned the *Joseph F. Fay* toward shore near Forty Mile Point Lighthouse. In no time, the vessel grounded onto the beach and turned sideways, the breakers pounding it. Slick as can be, the steep waves lifted the captain's quarters and wheelhouse from the deck and gently deposited them on the beach, still upright with men inside and one man asleep on a bunk. It was rumored the sleeping sailor never woke up. The barge, the *D.P. Rhoades*, came ashore four miles away.

The wrecked ship and barge are now on display in the county park near the beloved 1897 Forty Mile Point Lighthouse. It was saved by people forming the Forty Mile Point Lighthouse Society.

It has been said that no man sails upper Lake Huron without saying a blessing at the sight of the offshore Spectacle Reef Light, one the world's most famous lighthouses. Built in 1874 on a reef at the eastern end of the Straits of Mackinac, it defies ice floes, hurricane-force winds, and pounding waves.

Opening on May 1, 1897, Forty Mile Point Lighthouse, pictured above about 1900 and below in 2000, had a unique feature—room skylights—so at night keepers could check to see if the light was burning. The lighthouse is located between Presque Isle Light and Cheboygan Light and about 40 sailing miles from Mackinaw Point. Automated in 1969, Presque Isle County owns lighthouse, and the US Coast Guard maintains access to functioning light. A great museum is open from Memorial Day through October. (Above, USCG; below, AC.)

Described as the greatest engineering achievement in lighthouse construction on Lake Huron, the 1874 Spectacle Reef Lighthouse, pictured around 1880, was built 10 miles east of Bois Blanc Island over the most dreaded reef, which is feared by mariners. Work began in 1870 when a crib-dam was placed over the site. Three-foot bolts, pre-shaped stones from Marblehead, Ohio, and an 1871 invention—the strong-as-rock Portland Cement—turned the unique lighthouse into a construction marvel at that time. The five-story stone tower is hollow, with a room on each floor, and nearly 14 feet in diameter. The 93-foot tower held a Second Order Fresnel lens, flashing red and then white at 30-second intervals that was visible for 16.5 miles. Due to harsh conditions, only bachelors with dogs could be keepers. (NARA.)

In 1914, a puppy was swept away by the Milwaukee River. Engineer Albert Collins and machinist Clifford Perry from the lighthouse tender *Hyacinth*, servicing lighthouses, pulled the mixed-breed puppy from the river and gave it a future. Soon, Sport was a mascot and friend to everyone, and the *Hyacinth* became his home. For 12 years, Sport had a hand (or paw) in everything happening on the ship. He played ball and swam with the crew. When he died on July 19, 1926, he was given a burial at sea, and there was not a dry eye among those present. Capt. H.W. Maynard wrote a letter to Commissioner Putnam about Sport, describing him as "the best dog [he has] ever known." (AC.)

It seems strange that rugged lighthouse tenders with the toughest of men on board should be named after delicate flowers like marigolds or hyacinths. These ships and their fearless sailors went out on rough seas, taking lighthouse keepers to and from their lights—even during blizzards. A lighthouse tender is docked next to Spectacle Reef Light in this c. 1915 photograph. (NARA.)

In April 1902, keepers and dogs chop ice from the roof of the fog signal house at the opening of navigation at Spectacle Reef Lighthouse. Ice piled 30 feet high surrounded the lighthouse after the winter of 1873-1874 when the keepers first arrived. They had to cut their way in to gain entrance. (NARA.)

The Spectacle Reef Lighthouse Second Order Fresnel lens, pictured here, weighed almost four tons, including the pedestal and a rotating mechanism (not pictured). The interior diameter was a little over 55 inches. In 1972, the light was automated and the lens not needed, so members of the Great Lakes Historical Society in Vermilion raised money to save it. The huge lens was dismantled, packed into 44 crates, and reassembled at the museum. In 2012, the Great Lakes Historical Society will relocate from Vermilion to Toledo, and the lens will again be moved. (AC, GLHS.)

Notice the unusual shape of the small boat at Spectacle Reef Lighthouse. It was used to navigate among small chunks of ice on the lake before the water completely solidified. (NARA.)

The *Arthur M. Anderson*, pictured going through the Soo Locks in 1997, was following the *Edmund Fitzgerald* when the *Fitzgerald* sank on November 10, 1975, during a bad storm. Why did the *Anderson* survive and "the Fitz" did not? One of many theories surmises that the *Fitzgerald* struck bottom on the shallow Six Fathom Shoal, not unlike DeTour Reef, near Caribou Island and began taking on water. Captain Jesse Cooper of the *Anderson* was talking with Captain Ernest McSorley of the *Edmund Fitzgerald* during the storm. Later, men on the *Arthur M. Anderson*, watching the radar screen, saw the blip of the Fitz disappear when it went down. (AC.)

Rocky shoals extend from DeTour Point into the lake, causing ships to "detour" around the reef. Located where St. Mary's River flows into Lake Huron, it is a turning point for ships going through the Straits of Mackinac. First operated in 1848, DeTour Point Light was a white stone tower with 13 Argand lamps. In 1861, a new lighthouse was built, pictured here. (NARA.)

The 1931–1932 DeTour Reef Lighthouse, pictured here, was unusual. Built at end of the reef, it had a Diaphone foghorn with two signals: one for a foggy lake and one for a foggy lake and river. Cold water from the St. Mary's River mixed with the warmer water of Lake Huron and commonly caused foggy conditions. The lighthouse sits on a 60-square-foot concrete and steel crib. The spiral staircase, Fresnel lens, iron lantern, and pedestal room came from an old light. In 1974, the light was automated; in 1988, the lens was removed; in 1996, a new optic lens was installed. In 1998, residents of DeTour Village and Drummond Island formed DeTour Reef Light Preservation Society (DRLPS) to save and restore the light. (Above, NARA; below, USCG.)

Four

A MYSTERY AMONG ALPENA AREA LIGHTHOUSES

Put into use in 1840, the Old Presque Isle Lighthouse, with its hand-carved stone steps, rough brick walls, and antique, black chain hand rails, is reminiscent of New England–style structures.

In 1868, the 30-foot light was doused and abandoned. Later, men purchased the old light, restored it, and gave it another life as a historical attraction. By 1977, George and Loraine Parris ran a museum in the keeper's house next to the lighthouse. Years later, the darkened lens began to rotate and cast a light. This was a problem for captains whose navigational charts indicated there was no light in that area. So, US Coast Guard personnel again visited the lighthouse and disconnected the electricity and rotator mechanism.

In 1992, shortly after George passed away, the light began mysteriously glowing at night. So, Loraine Parris and her daughter covered the lens with a black blanket and then black plastic, but neither worked. The Coast Guard decided to change the angle of the lens. Occasionally, a "ghost" still lights the beacon, but Lorraine does not worry anymore. She believes the "spirit" is her deceased husband, an electrician, trying to take care of her and the light they both loved. Ghosts or no ghosts, many people have spent time trying to extinguish a light that supposedly is not there.

Old Presque Isle Lighthouse, pictured restored, was sold to Edward O. Avery in 1897 and then to Bliss Stebbins in the 1920s. Francis B. Stebbins, Bliss's brother, purchased the property in 1930 and restored it as a museum. In 1973, the lighthouse was added to the National Register of Historic Places. The property was then sold to the State of Michigan for a state park. The township historical society now operates the lighthouse as a museum from May through October. (AC.)

The lighthouse keeper climbed 45 unusual stone steps up the 30-foot tower at the Old Presque Isle Lighthouse. (AC.)

The most famous of all Great Lakes lighthouse families began their work in 1864 during the Civil War when President Lincoln appointed Patrick Garraty keeper of the Old Presque Isle Lighthouse. When the lighthouse was replaced by a 113-foot-tall tower a mile away in 1871, Garraty and his family moved to the new Presque Isle Lighthouse, seen on this page in the 1990s. Retiring in 1885, Garraty's son Thomas replaced him, who in turn retired in 1935. Thomas's brother Patrick lit his last beacon at St. Clair Flats after 50 years; another brother, John, was keeper for 25 years on various Lake Huron lights; and sister Anna was keeper for 23 years at the Presque Isle Range Lights. (At right, AC; below, Walter P. Reuther Library, Wayne State University.)

The Old Presque Isle Lighthouse is pictured here in 1940s. (Walter P. Reuther Library, Wayne State University.)

Dan and Marianne McGee were so upset by the deterioration of the lighthouse in 1985 that they formed the nonprofit Presque Isle Lighthouse Historical Society and leased the building from the US Coast Guard. Members of the society have spent years renovating the lighthouse. To raise money, they operate a gift shop and offer tours to the top of the tower, where a spectacular view of Presque Isle can be seen. In 1998, the US Coast Guard transferred the deed to Presque Isle County. (NARA.)

Presque Isle Lighthouse has its own rewards for those who visit. A museum invites the inquisitive, climbing the tower lures the active, a gorgeous setting tempts the curious, and the lighthouse seduces the romantic. (NARA.)

This 36-foot Chris-Craft cabin cruiser, seen in a 1940s postcard, was built at Algonac, Michigan. The L in "Alpena" marks the Presque Isle Lighthouse, and the A depicts the Alpena Light. (AC.)

In 1877, the Alpena Light, pictured on a wooden crib, replaced an 1875 temporary pole light with a lantern at the top. A disaster struck on July 12, 1888, when high winds fueled a fire that nearly consumed Alpena. Lumber stacked on the riverbank went up in smoke along with 200 homes, the pier, and the Alpena Light. It was rebuilt in 1888. (USCG.)

"This is some lumber town, lumber piles everywhere and [it] is a nice little city," wrote a person named C.C. on the back of this postcard of Alpena in the 1920s. Notice the stacks of lumber on the riverbank waiting to be shipped. (AC.)

In 1957, locals dubbed the unusual Alpena Light "Sputnik" since it resembled the Russian satellite. The cast-iron, 80-foot skeletal light, pictured here, was built in 1914. There are no other lights like this one. It was painted red in 1950s for better visibility and was automated in 1974. (USCG.)

Marvin and Joy Theaut purchased Middle Island Lighthouse, located eight miles north of Alpena, in 1988 and organized the Middle Island Lighthouse Keepers Association in 1992 to save and restore the lighthouse. The first light had a Fourth Order Fresnel lens. In 1928, a Third Order Fresnel lens was installed, and the light was changed from red to flashing green. In 1939, the tower, which rises 71 feet, was painted white with a black band and then later white with red-orange band. The light was automated in 1961. (USCG.)

Transparent water exposes a graveyard of ancient shipwrecks blanketing the reefs around the Thunder Bay Island Lighthouse. The area was known to befuddle ship captains. Mysterious currents swirl around the island that can steer vessels onto the reefs. At times, captains approaching the island in fog, snow, or rain believing their ship will pass on the safe eastern side later discover that they are actually on the more perilous western side. Historical logbook postings reveal puzzled comments by those who have experienced this section of Lake Huron. The first Thunder Bay Island Lighthouse was built in 1831 but soon fell. A second 40-foot tower was lit in 1832 before being raised to 50 feet in 1857. A fog bell was installed in 1858, and the light was automated in 1983. In 1993, the Thunder Bay Island Lighthouse Preservation Society formed to restore the light, pictured above about 1900. (NARA.)

Five

A Burning Ship Rescue and Mid-Michigan Lighthouses

When the wooden steamship *Marine City* loaded shingles at Alcona City on August 27, 1880, it was rumored that three stowaways were in the cargo hold hoping for a free ride. They did not know it at the time, but their devious attempt would not go unpunished. Perhaps the penalty was extreme for what they had done, but their fateful decision would be a permanent one. The ship left the dock and steamed for two hours. Approaching the Sturgeon Point Lighthouse, flames sprouted on the deck, licking at the smokestack. Panicked passengers moved toward the railing as fire quickly spread throughout the old wooden structure. Black smoke poured into the sky.

Capt. Thomas Hackett of the tugboat *Vulcan* saw the burning ship and steamed at top speed to the rescue. After arriving, the crew risked their lives, pulling survivors from the flaming wreck.

The rescue was considered a success, at least for the 121 passengers and crew onboard the *Marine City* who were saved. Believed to have died in the fire, the stowaways paid the ultimate price.

Wealthy Detroit brewers Mr. and Mrs. Voigt, grateful for their rescue, later presented gold and silver watches to crew of the *Vulcan* and a special gold medal to Capt. Thomas Hackett.

A deadly reef just offshore prompted construction of the 1869 Sturgeon Point Lighthouse, pictured above in 1904 and below in 2010. The tower is 68 feet high, and the original lens, a 3 1/2 Order Fresnel, came from an Oswego, New York, lighthouse. In 1939, the light was automated and the property deeded to State of Michigan in 1961. Sturgeon Point Light Station was later purchased and restored by the Alcona City Historical Society. An excellent museum in the keeper's dwelling is open Memorial Day through the end of autumn. (Above, NARA, below, AC.)

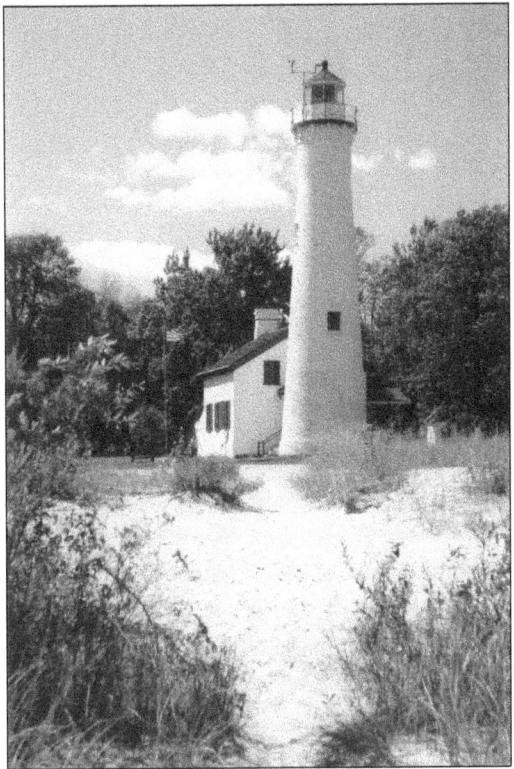

Several shipwrecks have occurred over the years at the Sturgeon Point Lighthouse, pictured here. In October 1887, the 233-ton schooner *Venus* struck nearby rocks and sank. In 1903, the three-masted schooner *Ishpeming* floundered, and a tugboat rescued the crew. In September 1924, the *Clifton*, loaded with stone, disappeared in a fierce storm, the wreckage floating to shore near the lighthouse. (AC.)

Land buildup created distance between Tawas Point Lighthouse and Lake Huron, so the first 1853 lighthouse had to be rebuilt in 1876 (pictured above about 1900). Currently, a 67-foot tower marks the northern entrance to Saginaw Bay. A two-and-half-story duplex was moved to the station in 1922 (pictured below in 2000) and removed in 2002. (Above, NARA; below, AC.)

A shipwreck mysteriously appears when sands shift near the Tawas Point Lighthouse, pictured here. The schooner *May Queen* was shipwrecked on a sandbar at Tawas Point, or Ottawa Point, on November 27, 1859. The crew was saved, but the schooner was lost. The reflection of Tawas Point and Lake Huron is revealed in this Fourth Order Fresnel lens, pictured at the Tawas light. Installed in 1891, it is still in use, but an electric motor now rotates the lens, and a 200,000-candlepower lightbulb casts a flashing white light, visible for 16 miles. (AC.)

Circular steps lead to the lantern room inside the Tawas Point Lighthouse. (AC.)

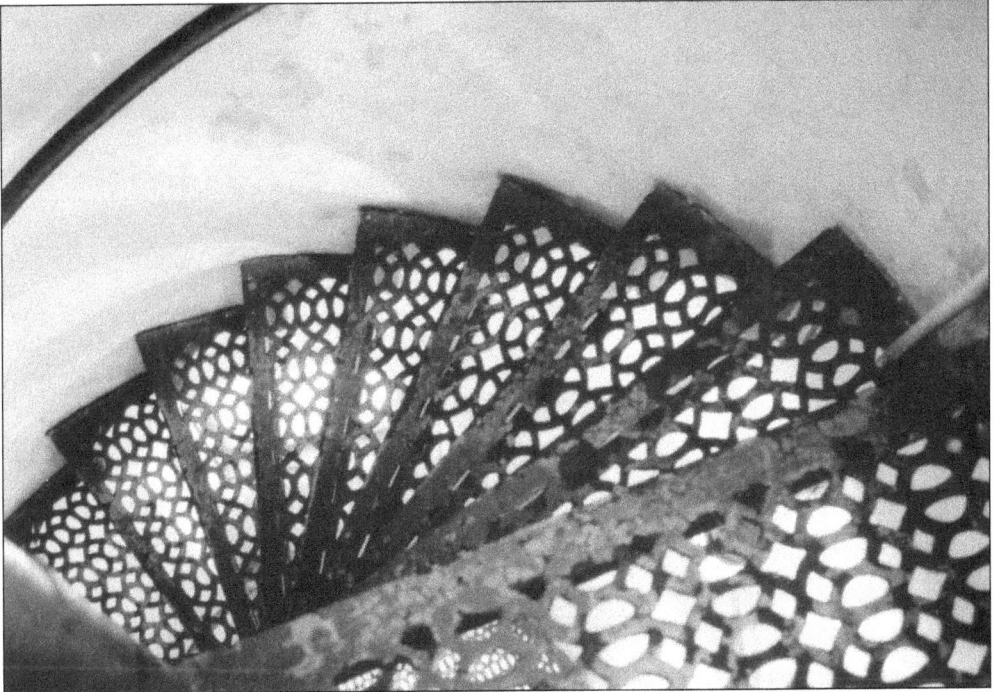

This photograph of Tawas Point Lighthouse was taken after 1899 since telephone lines run from dwelling to the fog signal. A concrete wall has replaced the original timber cribbing around the station. (Michigan State Archives.)

Tawas Point Lighthouse is pictured restored after 2003. It was added to the National Register of Historic Places in 1984. The station is still owned and operated by the US Coast Guard. (AC.)

In 1841, the 65-foot, rubble stone Saginaw Bay Lighthouse was built; range lights replaced it in 1876. The large Saginaw River Rear Range Light is pictured about 1890 (right) and about 1930 (below). The light was painted white in 1898 for better visibility, and a concrete pier was added in 1915. (At right, NARA; below, USCG.)

The 25-ton, 61-foot-tall steel Gravelly Shoal Lighthouse tower is being placed onto its crib in 1939. It replaced the Charity Island Lighthouse and is identical to the Huron and Conneaut towers in Lake Erie. Needing no lantern room, the light was automated at the top with an optic flashing every five seconds. A radio beacon was added later. (At left, NARA; below, USCG.)

Six

LIGHTHOUSES DURING THE "WHITE HURRICANE"

"Here we were in a deadly mess, a blinding blizzard blowing 80 miles per hour and we're unable to turn the ship away from danger," Captain Iler of the *George C. Crawford* told a reporter after surviving the historic November 13, 1913, storm, know as the "White Hurricane." He continued:

I passed the Fort Gratiot Lighthouse on Sunday at 3:15 a.m. [November 9, 1913]. Wind light, weather cloudy. At 10:20 a.m. I passed the Pointe aux Barques Lighthouse. By 4:00 p.m. the sea was running so high and the wind so strong that we were making no headway at all. . . . At 4:30, it got to be too much. . . . The blizzard was taking our breath away with roaring gusts—deafening, blinding. . . . I got the impression that the ship would not live for another hour in such a raging sea. . . . We couldn't see a thing. When we were running before the sea, the waves were so large they would fill up the stern of the ship and go over the very top of the cabin, down through the skylight, which was smashed through, and into the engine room. The waves broke all the windows in the cabin and filled the dining room and kitchen with water. . . . It snowed for a solid 26 hours, the minutes marked by the crash of breaking waves. I steered south by east for three hours, then south. I ran back 50 miles by log. . . . At 1:00 a.m. on Monday morning, we had soundings of 10 fathoms, and I realized with a bang that we must be below Sanilac [Lighthouse] in the pocket of Lake Huron and actually in serious danger. We either had to get turned around immediately or go ashore. . . . I ordered [a mate] to drop anchor. . . . Both anchors were on the bottom . . . about five minutes before they let go.

"We were in a . . . terrifying position. We had to fight it out," said Captain Iler. "I decided I would keep trying to turn around until she went on the beach. Then I could feel as if I had done all any man could have done to save his ship. . . . Our every nerve was on the alert watching for a clearing-up of the blizzard. Luck was with us. At 2:00 a.m., the wind shifted from north to northwest and a lull came with it. I got her headed north. We started back up the lake, and at noon on Monday, it had stopped snowing, and I was back abreast of Pointe aux Barques Lighthouse, which we had last seen 26 hours before. Next morning, going up Soo River [St. Mary's], we could see loose rivets and open joints. I never saw a gale to equal it." The Pointe aux Barques Lighthouse is pictured here in 1999. (AC.)

"No person on shore could have begun to realize the violence of the gale. It's a miracle that we got through, but we did, and without the loss of a man," said Almon T. Patchett, first mate of the *George C. Crawford*. He attributed their survival to the skill of Captain Iler during the "White Hurricane" of November 1913. During the storm, winds blew 60 to 70 miles per hour with spurts of 80 to 90 miles per hour. On Lake Huron, 188 lives and 24 ships were lost during the storm. The first 1847 Pointe aux Barques Lighthouse was replaced with a brick, 89-foot-tall light in 1857, pictured above. Today, a 1957 automated Twin DCB-224 Aero beacon casts a light. The cast-iron spiral stairs—103 steps to the lantern room—are pictured below. (Above, NARA; below, AC.)

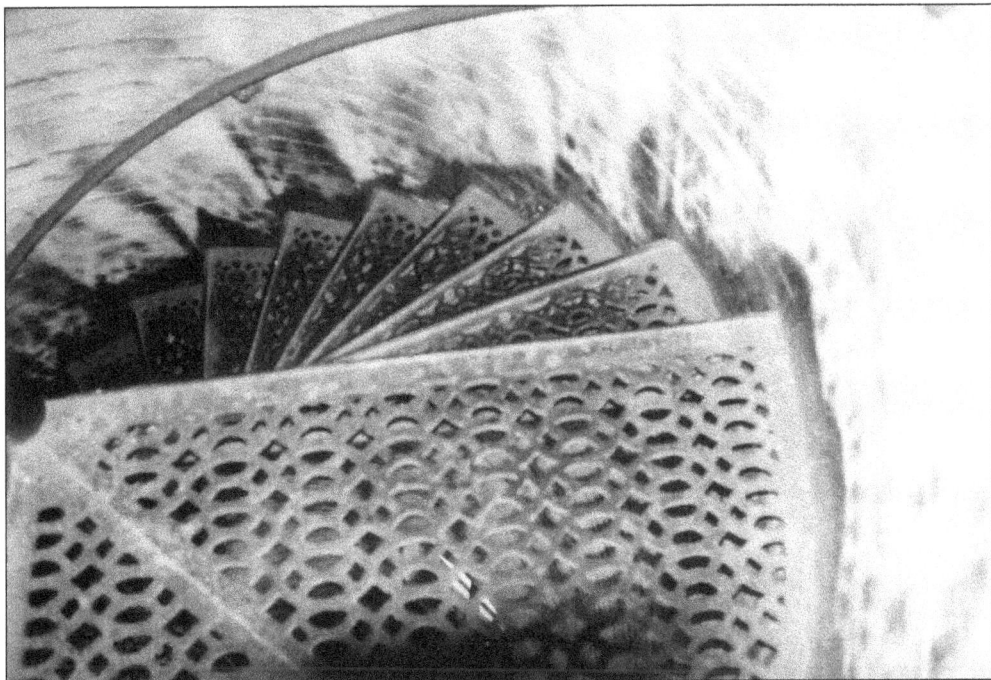

"The ship turned around into the trough and began to roll and tumble. We couldn't do anything," began Captain Hagen of the *Howard M. Hanna*, describing his fight with the November 13, 1913, storm. "We passed Fort Gratiot [Huron] Lightship at 5:12 a.m. Sunday, Harbor Beach Light at 11:30 a.m., Pointe aux Barques Light at 2:00 p.m. Then it started to snow heavily at 3:00 p.m. and we were facing tremendous waves. About 6:30 p.m. the bloody destruction began . . . doors and windows breaking, the icy water rushing into the engine room. . . . By 8:00 p.m., it was snowing so hard we couldn't see land, but we were about 15 miles off Pointe aux Barques Light. Shortly before 10:00 p.m. we could see Port Austin Light and knew we were dangerously close to Port Austin Reef. We dropped anchors but ship drifted broadside onto the reef and split in two. We clung to boat. On Tuesday, a few men took our one lifeboat to shore. Men from Port Austin Lifesaving Station saved the others on November 15, 1913." The Pointe aux Barques Lighthouse is pictured here. (AC.)

64

Battling a blizzard on November 26, 1966, the freighter *Daniel J. Morrell* passed near Pointe aux Barques Lighthouse, pictured here, when a crack developed in the center of the ship. With each pounding wave, the crack grew wider, and the vessel began to literally split in two. Arcs of blue and yellow lights flashed like lightning between the two sections from broken electric wires. The ship's front half sank quickly. With its propellers turning, the lighted rear of the freighter sped off into the night, going several miles before cold water hit the boilers, and the ship exploded. Four men in the water from the forward half of the ship climbed onto a raft. Four days later, at 4:00 p.m., helicopters spotted the snow and ice covered raft. Dennis Hale, near death, was the only survivor. (AC.)

Port Austin, a village in Huron County and on the shores of Lake Huron, was named after P.C. Austin, who started first lumber mill here in 1838. Lumber is being loaded onto a train in this 1925 photograph. (AC.)

A rocky reef 1.7 miles northwest of Pointe aux Barques was a threat to ships going into Saginaw Bay, so Port Austin Reef Lighthouse was built on September 15, 1878. A timber-framed tower, 57 feet tall, held a cast-iron lantern and a Fourth Order Fresnel lens. The lighthouse, pictured in 1895, is flanked by two wood-framed buildings that house steam engines for twin fog sirens, added in 1882. (NARA.)

The 60-foot Port Austin Reef Lighthouse, rebuilt in 1899 and pictured in 1933, was 16 feet square with double walls. The first floor contained the kitchen and dining area, and the other three floors held the living quarters and the office. The lens from the old tower was visible for 16 miles. Three feet of concrete facing was added to eight sides of the pier to protect it. The light was automated in 1953. The US Coast Guard wanted to demolish it in 1984. To save it, Louis Shillinger started the nonprofit Port Austin Reef Light Association in 1988. (USCG.)

An unidentified freighter hit the rocks and sank in the shallow channel in early 1950s. (AC.)

People were "thinking big" in 1873 with visions of a huge harbor in Lake Huron at Sand Beach. In rough weather, boats could take refuge in this man-made harbor. It was a good idea but became a major project over the years. Completed 12 years later, the two piers totaled 8,000 feet. An opening in the piers needed a light tower so boats could enter the harbor at night. A timber-framed open tower was built in 1875. It stood 44 feet above lake level with a fixed white light visible for 13 miles. In 1881, eight more cribs were added, and the breakwater pier was 5,205 feet long. In 1882, ships using the harbor totaled 1,000. On October 1, 1885, a new, prefabricated cast-iron Harbor Beach Lighthouse, seen here in 1900, replaced the old light. (NARA.)

Harbor Beach Lighthouse, identical to the Detroit River Lighthouse, is pictured above in 1885. It marked the entrance to 650-acre Sand Beach Harbor of Refuge, completed in 1885 and nicknamed "Million Dollar Harbor," as the cost to construct it was $1,205,781. The first floor contained a kitchen and dining area, the second and third floors were living quarters for keepers, and the fourth floor was a work area and watch room. The lighthouse was originally dark brown but was repainted white in 1900. A peaceful Michigan beach scene, one that both light keepers and sailors hope for when operating on the Great Lakes, is captured below. (Above, NARA; below, AC.)

Port Sanilac Lighthouse has a unique, elegant design. An octagonal brick tower 14 feet in diameter tapers to 9 feet, and bricks are laid like an upside-down staircase to support the gallery at the top. The Fourth Order Fresnel lens, lit on October 20, 1886, was visible for 13 miles. Richard W. Morris, the assistant keeper at Thunder Bay Island Light, was the first keeper until 1893, when William H. Holmes replaced him. The light was electrified in 1924 and automated in 1925. Although Holmes died in 1926, his widow, Grace, was the keeper until 1928 when the job was eliminated. (At left, USCG; below, AC.)

Seven

AN UNHAPPY KEEPER AND ST. CLAIR LIGHTHOUSES

In 1825, the Fort Gratiot Lighthouse keeper's job was a very desirable, government-appointed position. George McDougall, a Detroit lawyer, called on his influential friends, and they came through, appointing him as the first keeper.

Yet this lighthouse keeper's position was not the cushy job it appeared to be. The lighthouse was not built to government specifications, and the materials used were so inferior that George McDougall feared it would collapse. He refused to stay in the lighthouse at night. The keeper's dwelling, the free residence, was just as bad. The basement flooded constantly, so nothing could be stored there and the foul-smelling odors of the water permeated the house.

McDougall tried to make the best of a tough situation. He often spent his own money to make the house livable, but it seemed like a never-ending problem. As fast as McDougall's savings poured from the bank into house maintenance, the St. Clair River poured its water into the basement, cracking the walls. It was a losing battle.

The lighthouse was so rickety and unstable that it moved through various stages of collapse until it finally gave in to the elements and "died" four years after it was built. McDougall's savings collapsed about the same time as the lighthouse and residence.

"I have been master of boats for 21 years but this was the worst storm [on November 9, 1913] I have ever encountered. We were lucky to have survived," began Captain A.C. May of *H.B. Hawgood*, talking to a journalist. "Coming down Lake Huron we saw the *Price*, heading into the storm. It was beginning to blow so hard that I had turned the *Hawgood* and was heading for the [St. Clair] River. The freighter *Regina* was passed 15 miles south of Sand Beach [Harbor of Refuge]. The vessel *Scott* was met about 3:30 p.m. Sunday, with seas breaking over her, six miles north Port Huron [Fort Gratiot] Lighthouse. She was going up Lake Huron and I thought her Captain was foolish to leave the river." The Fort Gratiot Lighthouse is pictured above in 1891 and below in 1902. (Above, NARA; below, AC.)

"I would have given anything to have been past Fort Gratiot Lighthouse and inside shelter," continued Captain May of the *Hawgood*. "Wind and sea kept increasing and snow got thicker. We couldn't tell how it was blowing, but it was about 75 miles per hour from north-northeast. It got so thick we could not see the smokestacks. If we kept on we would have struck the beach. I wanted to save the boat, so we dropped anchors. Although I couldn't see I knew within a mile or two of where we were. My worry was some of the crew would be washed overboard. The anchors did not hold and we went on the [Wees] beach [the Canadian shore of Lake Huron]. We went on so hard I almost went through the pilot house when we struck. That was 10:00 p.m. Sunday night. We survived. They tell me that the freighters *Price*, *Regina*, and *Scott* were never seen again." The Fort Gratiot Lighthouse is seen in 1873 with the first keeper's house. (NARA.)

"I have seen many storms on the Great Lakes but never in my life as a sailor have I witnessed such a one as Sunday," said Capt. Thomas W. Carney to a reporter from the *Port Huron Times-Herald* on November 10, 1913. "We left Port Huron and Fort Gratiot Light at 1:00 a.m. Sunday morning bound from Buffalo to Milwaukee with a load of coal. Not until Saginaw Bay was reached at noon Sunday did the vessel encounter the severe storm. At this time the waves were as high as mountains, and breaking over the entire length of the boat. I did not want to take a chance of turning the big steamer *H.W. Smith* around in the trough of the sea and kept her headed with the engine steadily working. Finally, the wind blew at such terrific velocity and the sea became so heavy that the steamer became unmanageable. It was a critical moment. For a time the big boat wallowed helplessly in the trough of the sea and the waves tossed her about like a shell." The Fort Gratiot Lighthouse is pictured about 1900. (NARA.)

"After working desperately for an hour or more, the crew and I got the boat under control and turned down the lake," continued Captain Carney. "With the waves dashing so furiously, the *Smith* made slow progress towards Fort Gratiot Light," pictured here about 1920. "Tons of water poured down the ship's decks and she reeled heavily. As the storm increased, it seemed improbable that the boat would be able to weather the gale. Heavy seas crushed in the windows of the pilothouse and the crew was compelled to seek shelter in the after cabin, which was also partially wrecked. Throughout the night the crew fought the elements and as the waves broke down the doors and windows, temporary barricades were erected. Clothing, provisions, and furnishings were swept overboard and the crew was doubtful of ever again reaching port. But Luck was with us." (Walter P. Reuther Library, Wayne State University.)

Standing five feet, nine inches tall and weighing 200 pounds, George McDougall, the first official Fort Gratiot Lighthouse keeper, liked to eat and drink both on and off the job. Anyone who has climbed tiny lighthouse steps to the top and tried to squeeze through a small opening into the lantern room will understand McDougall's complaints about the narrow stairway and small opening, 18 inches by 21.5 inches, to the lantern room. It was rumored that he only squeezed into the lantern room once and ascended the stairway sideways. He hired an assistant to tend the lighthouse, pictured here. Friends also appointed him postmaster and customs inspector, positions he held until his death in 1842. (AC.)

Fort Gratiot Lighthouse was built in 1825, then collapsed, and was rebuilt in 1829. The height was increased from 74 feet to 86 feet in 1861, a brick duplex was added in 1874, and a retaining wall was built after the 1913 "White Hurricane" storm undermined the foundation. The light, pictured here, was automated in 1933. (AC.)

In formal evening wear, 1,400 passengers boarded the *Tashmoo* for a romantic moonlit cruise on June 18, 1936, but an accident prevented the ship from ever returning. The *Tashmoo* left Detroit on a 25-mile trip south to Sugar Island and back. People danced to soft music from a live band, and couples moved to the ship's rail to steal a kiss. After rounding Grosse Ile, Capt. Donald McAlpine felt the ship shudder. Engineers reported a hole in the bottom and the ship taking on water. It was 11:45 p.m. (AC.)

Captain McAlpine of the *Tashmoo* instructed the crew to say nothing to any of the passengers of the leak, only to tell them the ship was going to make a stop at Amherstburg, Canada, for engine repairs. He instructed the band to keep playing, the drinks to keep flowing, and the food to continue to be served. He turned the ship toward Canada—it was a race against time. The ship steamed on, full speed ahead. At midnight, the *Tashmoo* pulled to the Amherstburg dock. Laughing and singing, the passengers began to depart, and no one noticed the ship sinking. When all the passengers were on shore, the captain told them the truth. Laughing and cheering, they thanked him for saving everyone and considered him a hero. Above, the *Tashmoo* leaves a Detroit dock with passengers in 1911 and below proceeds up the Detroit River in 1900s. (AC.)

Steamer Tashmoo.

Captain and crew agreed that a submerged boulder gouged a hole in the *Tashmoo*. It was speculated river currents moved the boulder into the channel. An error made during the salvage operation broke the keel, and the ship was scrapped after 36 years of service. The photograph above shows the *Tashmoo* docked behind the *City of Alpena*. Both ships were loading passengers at the White Star Line Dock in Port Huron in 1905. Before 1919, the *City of Alpena* made the round-trip voyage from Toledo, Ohio, to St. Ignace, Michigan, each week with 10 stops. (AC.)

At Port Huron, electric-powered engines enter St. Clair Tunnel, heading to Canada, in 1912. Steam-powered engines originally were used, but several accidents occurred between 1892 and 1904, and 10 men were asphyxiated from the fumes in the accidents. (AC.)

St. Clair Flats Front (above) and Rear Range (below) Lights were built in 1859 between Gull Island and the southwestern end of Harsen's Island to guide ships into the St. Clair River from Lake St. Clair. The front light had a focal plane of 28 feet, and its Fifth Order Fresnel lens was a fixed white light with a 10-mile radius. The rear range light, 1,000 feet behind, had a focal plane of 44 feet, and its Fourth Order Fresnel lens was a fixed white light beaming 12 miles. The keeper's house was attached to the rear range light. In 1907, the lights became obsolete. In 1988, Chuck Brockman began the Save Our South Channel Lights (SOSCL). (USCG.)

L.T. Discontinued: Close Navig. 1907

St Clair Flats Range. Rear. 1904

HURON AVE LOOKING NORTH PORT HURON, MICH.

Out for a drive on March 26, 1922, Mr. and Mrs. William Smith, with their son and daughter, planned on eating at home on Quay Street in Port Huron at 2:00 p.m., but their car became stuck in a dirt road—and it saved their lives. Their home was 300 feet from the Black River ferry docks. At 2:20 p.m. the ferryboat *Omar D. Conger* (pictured above in 1905) exploded, sending a 25-ton steam boiler crashing into their house; the resulting fire consumed everything. While preparing the ship for launch, chief engineer Campbell and fireman Althouse were firing up the boilers when the blast occurred. Low water in the boilers may have caused the explosion that killed four on board. (AC)

Port Huron, Michigan - Black River.

A lighthouse keeper and his family pose in front of a St. Clair Flats Canal Lighthouse around 1890. (NARA.)

In July 1871, a wider, straighter channel into the St. Clair River was dredged near Harsen's Island (pictured here). It was 20 feet deep, 300 yards wide, and a mile to a mile and a half long. The dredged bottomlands were piled into two-mile-long islands surrounding the channel called the St. Clair Flats Ship Canal. Metal seawalls contained the mile-long dike. (AC.)

Twin lighthouses, the St. Clair Flats Ship Canal Upper Light (above in 1891) and the Lower Light (below), were built at each end of the two-mile-long islands surrounding the canal in 1871. The identical lighthouses were 45 feet tall and had an oil house, a boathouse, and indoor plumbing. In 1906, a canal was dredged on the west side of the island for down-bound ship traffic to use. Up-bound traffic used the east side of original canal. In the 1930s, lighthouses and islands were destroyed, and a wider channel was dredged for ships. (NARA.)

In 1934, the US Lighthouse Service built skeletal range light towers on the south end of Harsen's Island to guide ships from Lake St. Clair into the St. Clair River. A one-and-a-half-story keeper's house was built next to the largest light, called the Harsen's Island Lights, in the St. Clair Flats. From 1935 to 1939, the new "robot" lightship *St. Clair* was operated from this station. (USCG.)

The Lake St. Clair Crib Light, pictured here, replaced the St. Clair Lightship in 1939. (USCG.)

Eight

SECRETS OF SLIGHTLY SINFUL LIGHTHOUSES

During Prohibition, the *London Times* (of Ontario, Canada) exposed how some law-abiding citizens were engaging the illegal activity of distributing and selling alcohol. People in Canada brought liquor to the banks of the Detroit River and hid in trees and tall grass. As smugglers' boats passed by, those on land signaled to them with small torches. The boaters would then stop on shore and bargain for the liquor. After a deal was made, the alcohol was loaded onto the boat and taken across the river to the American side, where it was hidden in bushes. Rowboats had the advantage of silence, but they did not have enough speed to get away if spotted by patrol boats.

People adopted their own pattern of light signals for "stop" and "go." On a dark night, the shoreline came alive with light signals, indicating a small, custom boat was starting across the river. Blue flashing lights meant an "all clear" sign, while red flashing lights warned of danger and law enforcement; a white sheet hung on a clothesline also meant police were in the area.

This new activity was called rum-running, and the Detroit River lighthouses played an important role in guiding these boats at night. They were also silent witnesses to more bizarre situations on the Detroit River than anyone could have imagined.

The impressive Belle Isle Lighthouse was built on the northern end of Belle Isle, an island in the middle of the Detroit River. Fancy trim gave it a classy look, and even when a circular iron oil house was added in 1891, it did not deter from the lighthouse's beauty. (NARA.)

Seen here on a hot day, Detroiters are enjoying the bathing beach and pavilion on Belle Isle near the lighthouse in the 1920s. (AC.)

Belle Isle Lighthouse opened on May 15, 1882, on the 700-acre Bell Isle in the Detroit River. White gingerbread trim, balconies on second-floor windows, and a black, wrought-iron fence made this Victorian lighthouse unique, seen here in an extremely rare, c. 1883 photograph. Detroit city leaders had visions of an elaborate park when they purchased Belle Isle in 1879 for $200,000. Eventually, $2 million would be spent for a zoo, horticultural center, casino, and park development. The light keeper's home included spectacular views from every window and the convenience of a fabulous park within walking distance. It was no wonder that the second lighthouse keeper, Louis Fetes Jr., stayed for 43 years (1886–1929) until the light was automated. (NARA.)

The first keeper of the 1882 Belle Isle Lighthouse, pictured here in 1937 from another angle, was William Badger, who left in 1885 to become keeper at Windmill Point Lighthouse at Grosse Point. During Prohibition, the Windsor-Detroit area around the Belle Isle Lighthouse was nicknamed "Rum Alley." It was estimated that 90 percent of the liquor brought illegally to Detroit came by boat. The nearby marshy Canadian shoreline boasted 50 floating "export docks." And it was said that a customs agent's payoff averaged $2,000 a week. (Walter P. Reuther Library, Wayne State University.)

Detroit's rich and successful elite docked their yachts at the prestigious Detroit Yacht Club on Belle Isle, pictured here in 1940. Sipping exotic drinks and savoring gourmet food, Detroit millionaires from the booming automobile industry mingled and played in this exclusive clubhouse. (AC.)

In April 1929, Capt. Joseph Burkheiser, harbormaster and commanding officer of the Belle Isle Police Station, was accused of using police boats and policemen to transport liquor from Canada to Detroit. As payment, he generously shared his alcohol with them. He was also caught storing booze at the Belle Isle Police Station. When it was revealed that the police were running liquor across the river, stunned citizens voiced opinions for and against Prohibition, while others laughed. Burkheiser was fined $500, reduced to a lieutenant, and forced retired. By 1929, the gingerbread trim was out of style and removed from the Belle Isle Lighthouse, pictured here. (Above, NARA; below, AC.)

People in Detroit are seen concealing liquor in baggage before Prohibition. Forbidden booze became much more tempting when the government said that no one could possess it. People who supported Prohibition, the "Drys," tried to make Prohibition look good and that the country was a better place with fewer saloons. People against Prohibition, the "Wets," tried to make the country look bad and that there were more gangsters. Government officials claimed they were successful in enforcing Prohibition to try and make themselves look good and to frighten Congress into giving them more money. And "politicians lied through force of habit," wrote historian Herbert Asbury, calling the 1920s the "era of the big lie." (Walter P. Reuther Library, Wayne State University.)

Cars, trucks, and boats, pictured in Detroit during Prohibition, were rebuilt with false roofs, hidden compartments under seats, and fuel tanks that would be filled with liquor. The best trick was to use hearses, which held liquor in closed caskets instead of the deceased. The truck pictured below appears to have runners for traveling over ice during the winter. (Walter P. Reuther Library, Wayne State University.)

Flat Foot, an awkward-looking, flat-bottom, 20-year-old fishing boat, similar to the one pictured here, began hauling illegal liquor in 1922 during Prohibition. Year after year, for seven years, she transported liquor from Canada to Detroit and Cleveland, making hundreds of trips across Lake Erie, and was never stopped. There was a standing order to capture the boat, with or without whiskey, but no one could. (USCG.)

Flat Foot's unusual luck became legend. She lost a rudder near West Sister Island during a terrible storm, and the crew abandoned her in a lifeboat; she survived the gale. The next day, another rumrunner found her and towed her into Kingsville, Ontario, along with her 90 barrels of beer. Another time, in a storm near Monroe, Michigan, *Flat Foot* ran within 20 feet of US Coast Guard vessel no. 142 going in the opposite direction. By the time the Coast Guard boat turned around, *Flat Foot* had disappeared in the dark. Pictured are Coast Guard–confiscated speedboats in Detroit that were not so lucky. (Walter P. Reuther Library, Wayne State University.)

The police were not naïve about what was happening during Prohibition. Carl Farrow, former chief of the Windsor Police Department and provincial constable from 1928 to 1934 in Amherstburg, explained, "People in rowboats would dock in Amherstburg, Canada, fill their small boats with whiskey, and clear for Cuba. Your destination had to be a port where you could import liquor. You knew they were not going there, they'd never make it. Anyway they'd leave and in a few hours they'd be back, the same people in the same boat. They would clear another load of liquor for Cuba and away they'd go past the Detroit River Lighthouse." The Detroit River Lighthouse, which witnessed quite a few of these runs, is pictured in 1885. (Walter P. Reuther Library, Wayne State University.)

Whiskey is loaded into railroad cars in Canada. After reaching the United States, men would throw cases of liquor from the train to men in buggies riding alongside. (Walter P. Reuther Library, Wayne State University.)

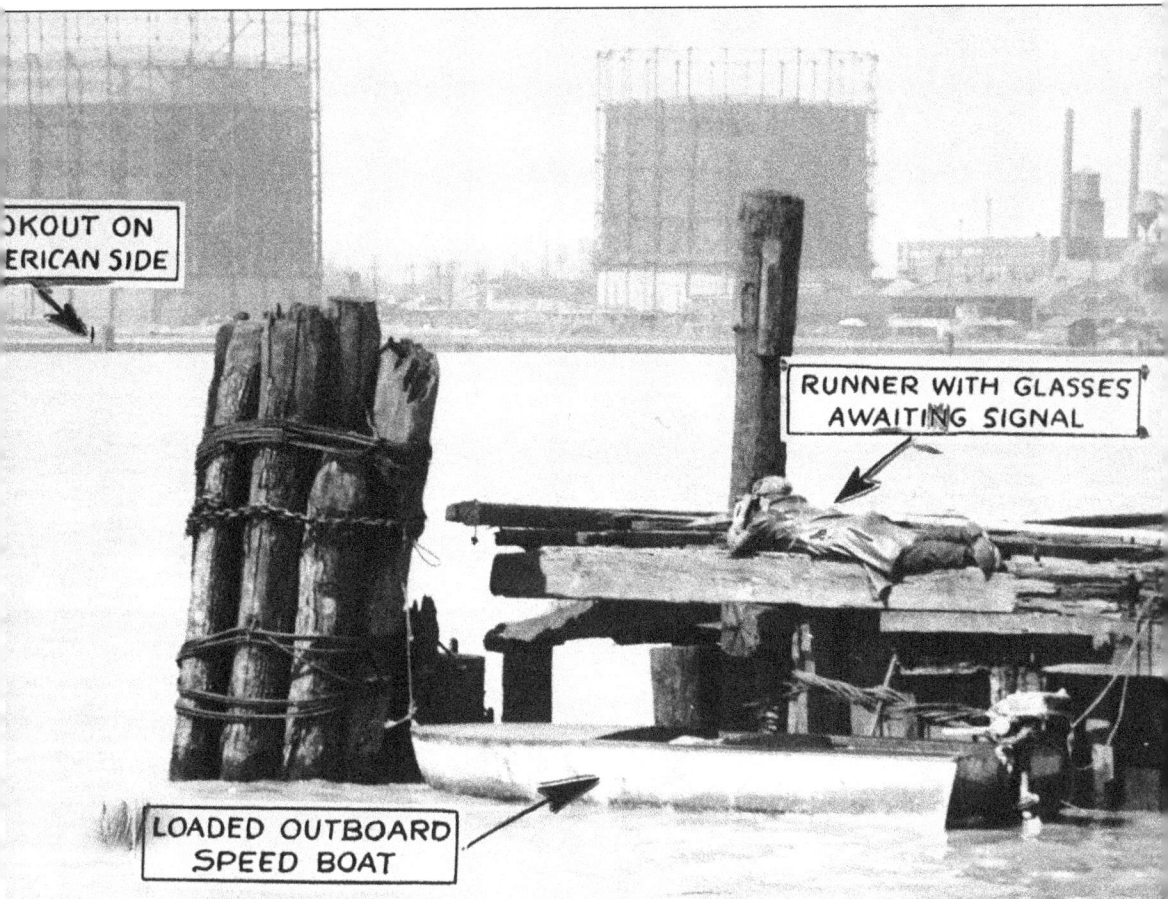

**)KOUT ON
ERICAN SIDE**

**RUNNER WITH GLASSES
AWAITING SIGNAL**

**LOADED OUTBOARD
SPEED BOAT**

A smuggler on a dock waits for a signal to cross the Detroit River. For 10 years, the border patrol, the police, and other inspectors got rich from payoffs while Prohibition agents looked the other way, and payoffs from rumrunners poured money into the community. But all of that changed in 1929, when a smooth-talking, likeable undercover agent infiltrated the border patrol and collected $1,700 in bribes. When this agent blew the whistle, the border patrol began to go down faster than a sinking ship in a Lake Erie storm. (Walter P. Reuther Library, Wayne State University.)

During the trial, the undercover agent explained how the payoffs worked. First, agents would be paid to look the other way for three or four hours while the liquor crossed the Detroit River before being paid again when it was moved to other cities. These "fixers" would tell agents when other rumrunners were going to cross the river so agents could catch them and put them out of business. When the testimony was over, it appeared that the border patrol personnel were going to jail, even though they pled "not guilty." The prosecution was confident of its case and certain of victory when the jury left for deliberations. Many people were openly breaking the liquor law, either drinking at "blind pigs"—speakeasies or illegal bars—or selling liquor from their homes, so there was sympathy for others doing the same. For years, people played both sides, as there was very little enforcement of the law. The smugglers are pictured in Detroit waiting for boat to bring whiskey. (Walter P. Reuther Library, Wayne State University.)

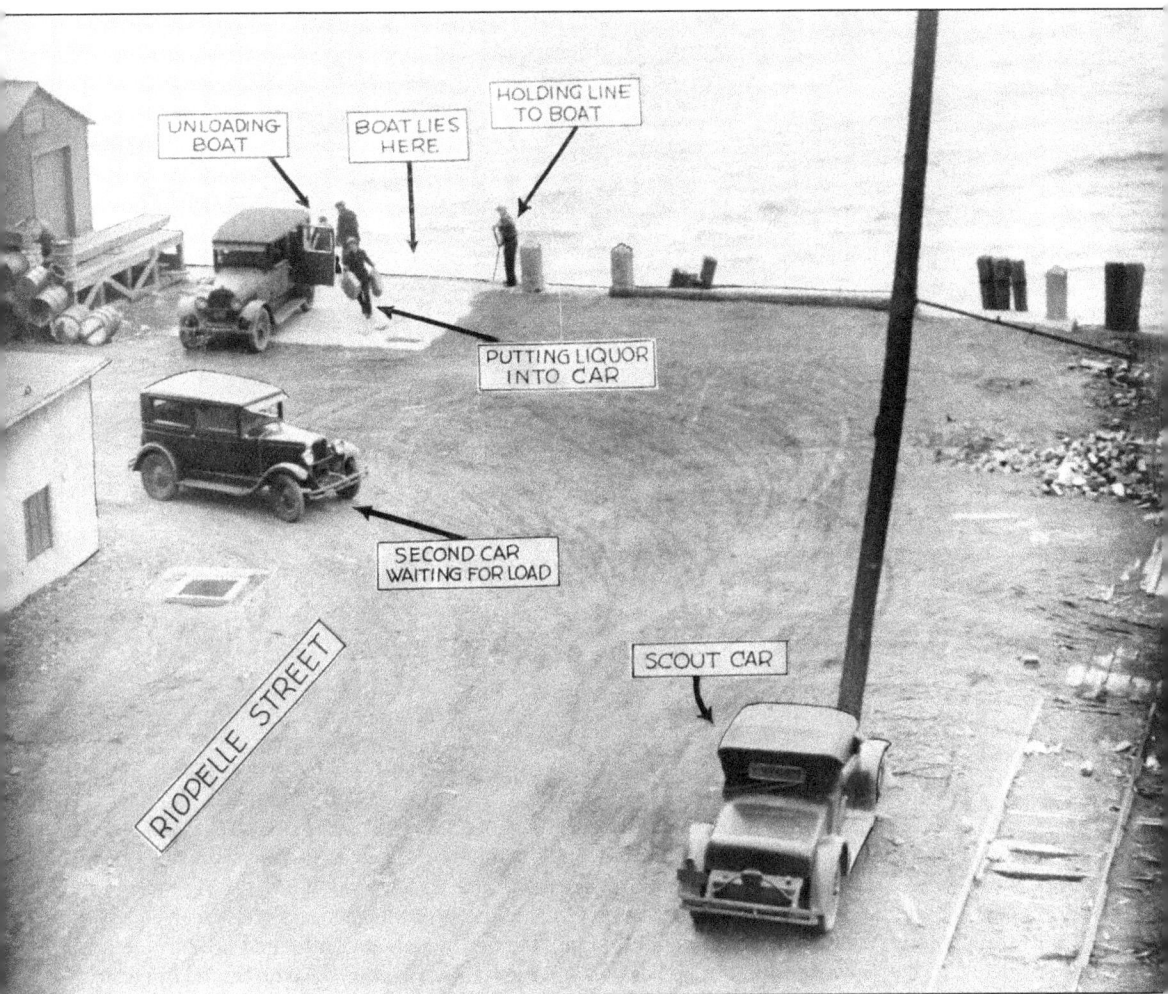

When the jury returned with a verdict, border patrol agents sat nervously contemplating their bleak future. The verdict was read, "For lack of sufficient evidence, the verdict is not guilty." The courtroom erupted like a volcano. Smiling friends and family hugged the defendants, the district attorney dropped his face in anger, and vocal complaints arose from teetotalers. This, among many other events, helped bring a repeal of Prohibition in 1934. (Walter P. Reuther Library, Wayne State University.)

During Prohibition, liquor flowed into Detroit, and the small bays and islands were a smuggler's dream come true. Detroit claimed it had 4,000 speakeasies, with dancing and food, during Prohibition. Owners of blind pigs, had to pay police to survive, and most government officials received payoffs. In the photograph above, police raid a blind pig. Pictured below, a confiscated boat in Detroit is loaded with liquor wrapped in burlap bags. (Walter P. Reuther Library, Wayne State University.)

A truck loaded with beer went through the ice on Lake St. Clair during Prohibition in 1933. Curious people from Gross Pointe have walked over the ice to get a closer look. During Prohibition, cars and trucks hauled liquor across Lake St. Clair and the Detroit River in the wintertime. Doors were removed so people could escape if the vehicle sank. Rumrunners also put sled runners under their boats, and several men wearing spiked shoes would pull them across the ice. Among the many tricks used to transport Canadian liquor across the river at night in the summertime involved two small boats, one pulling the other with a 2,000-foot rope. The line was fastened to the first boat below the surface, so if it was stopped no connection could be made to the far-off second boat loaded with the liquor. This method was used with much success. (Walter P. Reuther Library, Wayne State University.)

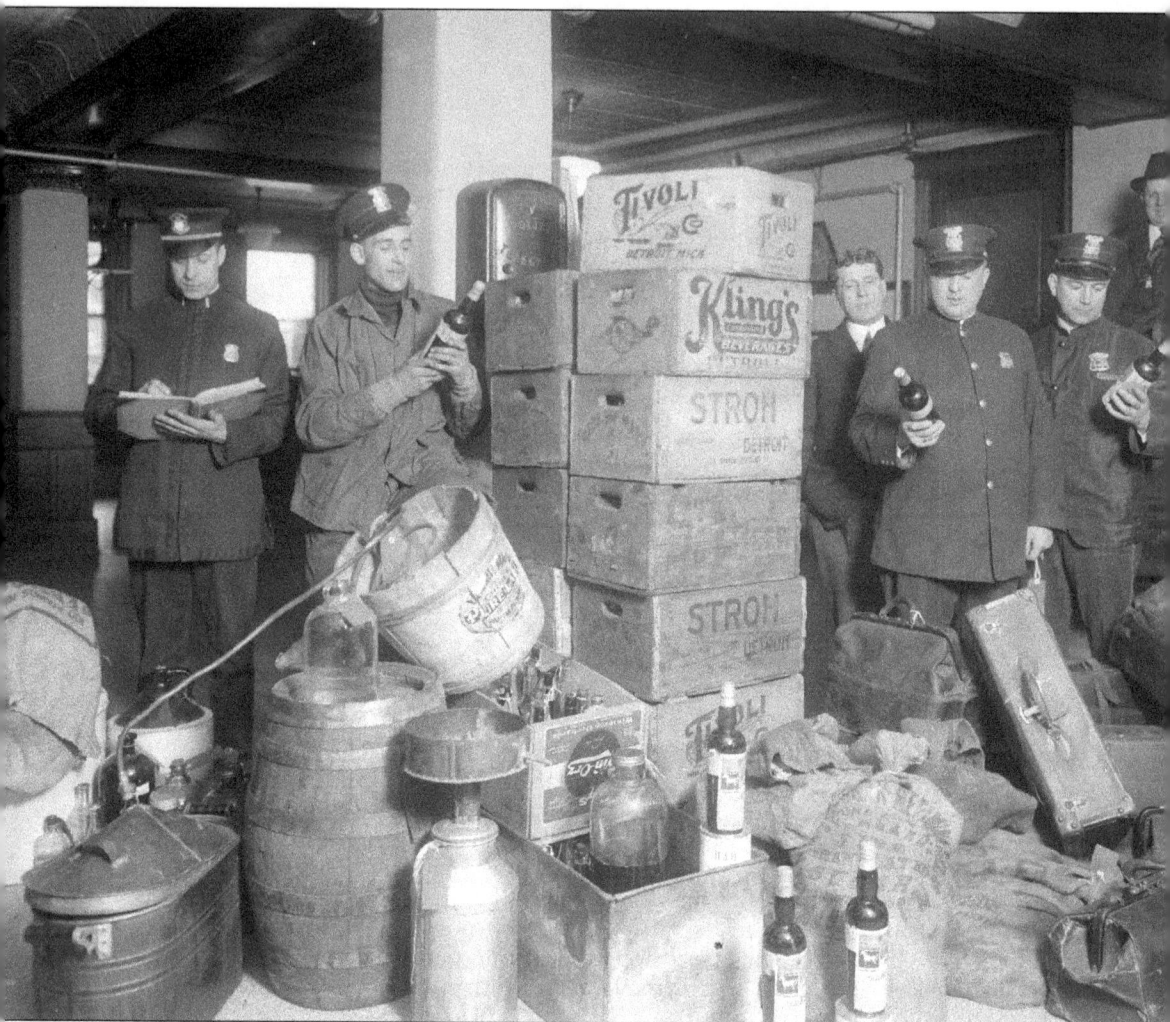

Elmer Holman, the secretary of the Lapeer chapter of the Anti-Saloon League, thought he could get away with selling booze. It was a good cover, and it worked for a while: protesting the sale of liquor during the day while making a bundle selling booze at night. On March 19, 1926, though, 400 angry townspeople stormed city council protesting the lack of liquor enforcement. Holman should have quit then, but he did not. Eventually, undercover agents nailed the two-timing Holman to the wall, testifying he sold three kinds of whiskey, two types of beer, four brands of wine, and "carrot champagne." Pictured is a police raid on a blind pig in Detroit. (Walter P. Reuther Library, Wayne State University.)

The Detroit River Lighthouse, put in operation in 1885, was painted white for better visibility by 1904. During Prohibition (1920–1934), the lighthouse helped rumrunners navigate at night from Amherstburg, Canada, to Monroe, Sandusky, and Toledo. This "spark plug" type tower marked the entrance to the Detroit River and warned sailors of the Bar Point Shoal that sank vessels in the 1870s. It was nicknamed "The Rock" by keepers. (NARA.)

ELECTRIC MOTOR EMERGING FROM EAST BOUND TUBE UNDER DETROIT RIVER WITH MICHIGAN CENTRAL TRAIN, DETROIT, MICH.

Seen in 1912, a train with an electric engine emerges from a two-mile 1910 tunnel under the Detroit River between Detroit and Windsor. These trains transported illegal liquor during Prohibition. (AC.)

Many rum boats had concealed storage areas. Fishermen buried bottles of whiskey under layers of ice and fish and were never caught. One boat, though, was unlucky. The story goes that after fish were removed and no liquor was discovered, suspicious Coast Guard personnel drove a heavy, steel-pointed rod through what seemed to be the bottom of the boat, but no water emerged. Extending the rod a few more feet, it came against the real bottom. He discovered a hidden compartment loaded with booze that was causing the ship to ride so low in the water. Pictured are confiscated rum boats in Detroit in 1928. (Walter P. Reuther Library, Wayne State University.)

During Prohibition, customs agents did not frisk working-class girls, so businessmen hired secretaries to bring liquor back from Canada on ferries, pictured here. Booze was hidden in lunch boxes and inside coat pockets. Also, bottles of liquor could be hung from a special belt and concealed under skirts and pants. The belt idea worked best unless the bottles clinked together while the person was standing in front of a customs agent. (AC.)

The Spray was a 30-foot cabin cruiser speedboat no one could catch, skimming the water at 35 miles per hour. During Prohibition, she acquired a reputation as the fastest rumrunner around Detroit, and both sides knew it. *The Spray* would slowly leave a Canadian dock in the Detroit River, even in daylight, the captain slowly steering the boat on the Canadian side of the river past the US Coast Guard boat, with guns visible, on the US side. When out of gun range and near Lake Erie and the Detroit River Lighthouse (pictured here in 1950), her skipper would push forward the throttle, the engine would roar like a lion, and away she would go, disappearing on the horizon. The US Coast Guard sometimes pursued the boat but would fall far behind and give up. Two years later, a US Coast Guard cutter caught her when her motor bearings burned. The engine was replaced and *The Spray* reversed its role and became a rumrunner's nightmare. (Walter P. Reuther Library, Wayne State University.)

The 1927 Canadian Livingstone Channel Lighthouse is pictured after the freighter *James Reed* collided with it. The light was located in the Detroit River above Amherstburg and mid-river between down-bound Livingston Channel and up-bound Amherstburg Channel. Keepers kept logbooks of passing freighters, and information was sent to a central Detroit office. The *J.W. Wescott II* delivered mail and ships' orders to passing vessels. Given a duplicate, lighthouse keepers delivered ships' orders to vessels if the *Wescott* could not. In September 1952, the 600-foot freighter *E.J. Kulas* collided with the lighthouse in the fog and destroyed it. A pole light replaced it until global positioning (GPS) became common, and the crib and light were removed. (Walter P. Reuther Library, Wayne State University.)

Above, a US Marine Postal Service mailman in a rowboat tosses a line up to a sailor on a moving 350-foot freighter in the Detroit River. Below, standing in rocking rowboat, a US Marine Postal Service mailman drops mail into a sailor's swinging bucket. These images were taken in the early 1900s. (AC.)

Nine

LOST LIGHTHOUSES
OF THE DETROIT RIVER

Years ago, Mama Juda Island disappeared in the Detroit River—its inhabitants, lighthouses, and fisheries forgotten. But a courageous, 14-year-old girl living there saved a life in 1890, and everyone remembered. Her name was Maebelle Mason, the lighthouse keeper's daughter. Capt. Montague, on the passing steamer *C.W. Elphiche*, signaled to the lighthouse keeper's family and told them a man was clinging to an overturned rowboat a mile up the river. Since lighthouse keeper Orlo J. Mason was away, Maebelle and her mother rowed their boat to the drowning man. Maebelle rescued the man, and they rowed back to the lighthouse with his overturned boat in tow.

Maebelle Mason was presented a silver lifesaving medal from the 10th Lighthouse District inspector and a gold lifesaving medal from the Shipmasters' Association. Inscribed on the medal: "Presented to Miss Maebelle Mason for heroism in saving life May 11, 1890, by E.M.B.A. of Cleveland." After the incident, ship captains always blew their steam whistles when they passed by the second Mama Juda Island Lighthouse, Maebelle's home. It was a simple gesture, but saving a life at sea was always important to captains and crew, for all of them wanted to believe that Maebelle, or someone like her, would come to their aid if they fell overboard and were struggling to survive.

The first 1849 Mama Juda Lighthouse, pictured at left on September 30, 1858, with a birdcage-style lantern room, marked the shoals near the north end of Grosse Ile and Wyandotte on the mainland. Rebuilt in 1866, the second Mama Juda Island Lighthouse, Maebelle's home, is pictured below. The lantern room contained a Fourth Order Fresnel lens with a fixed red light. A third Mama Juda Lighthouse, on the next page, was built in 1910. (NARA.)

Affluent people from Detroit, many from the booming auto industry like Horace Dodge, built elaborate estates and summer homes in the Grosse Point area, and a lighthouse here had to look the part. The new keeper's house was embellished with gingerbread trim to fit in with the ritzy neighborhood. The Windmill Point Lighthouse, put into operation in 1875 on the Grosse Pointe Park/Detroit border, replaced an earlier lighthouse dated to 1838. (Grosse Pointe Historical Society.)

The 1910 third Mama Juda Island Lighthouse washed away in 1920 when a freighter rammed it. Using rowboats, keepers also tended the Grosse Ile Lighthouse and channel lights. (Grosse Ile Historical Society.)

Windmill Point Lighthouse is pictured about 1910 with a larger keeper's house. Shorter, smaller range lights placed nearby in Lake St. Clair worked in conjunction with this tall light as the rear range beacon. (Walter P. Reuther Library, Wayne State University.)

Windmill Point Lighthouse, pictured being demolished in the 1930s, was sometimes called Grosse Pointe Lighthouse. It was a sad day when this gorgeous lighthouse was torn down. (Walter P. Reuther Library, Wayne State University.)

The 1908 Peche Island Rear Range Light, pictured in 1935, was saved because the people of Detroit cared about its future. It was leaning when it was deactivated in the 1960s, but it had friends. When the US Coast Guard was going to demolish it, members of the Michigan National Corporation of Detroit raised money to buy it. They saved the light and moved it to the banks of the Detroit River at Waterworks Park in Marine City, Michigan. (USCG.)

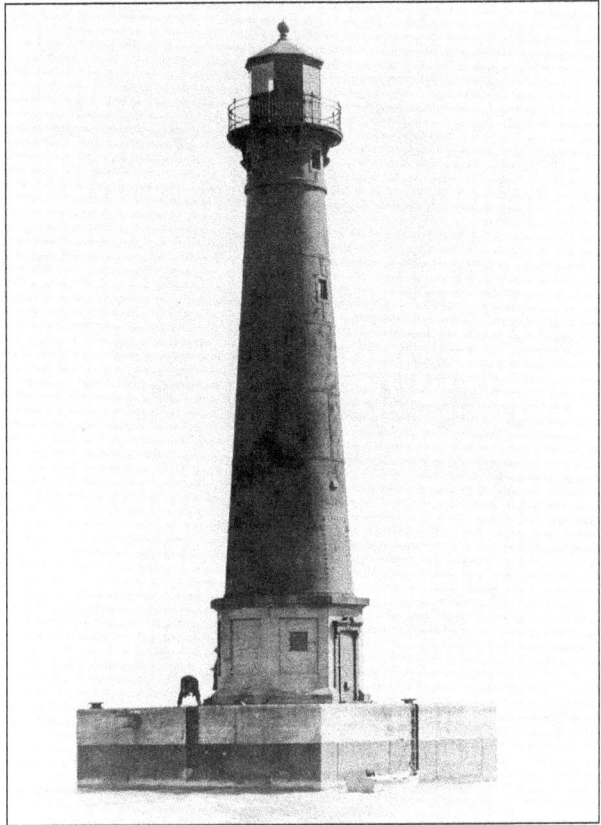

This rare c. 1920 photograph shows Peche Island Front Range Light in Lake St. Clair with its lighthouse keepers. (Walter P. Reuther Library, Wayne State University.)

The William Livingstone Memorial Lighthouse, put into operation in 1930, was privately financed and continues to be maintained by the Lake Carriers' Association and the citizens of Detroit in memory of the late William Livingstone. He pioneered the construction of the deep Livingstone Channel. The only marble lighthouse in the world greets freighters passing Belle Isle.

The 1891 Grosse Ile South Channel Rear Range Lighthouse is pictured here prior to being razed in the 1940s. Range lights in the area, since vanished, were tended by a lighthouse keeper who lived on Mama Juda Island. (Walter P. Reuther Library, Wayne State University.)

Climbing the Grosse Ile South Channel Rear Range Light took courage. A brave keeper poses by the light in the photograph above. The light collapsed three years after it was built during a storm on September 3, 1894. (NARA.)

The unusual 1894 Grosse Ile North Channel Rear Range Light, pictured, displayed a fixed white light. Automated in the 1920s, it was extinguished and destroyed in the 1960s. (USCG.)

Grosse Ile South Channel Front Range Light is pictured in 1894, the year it was put into service. (USCG.)

Today, the Grosse Ile North Channel Range Light is the only light that remains on Grosse Ile. Rebuilt in 1906, the interior includes varnished Michigan pine and a wooden circular staircase. An occulting (flashing) white beacon was extinguished in 1963. This beautiful lighthouse is maintained for all to enjoy by the Grosse Ile Historical Society. (Grosse Ile Historical Society.)

This September 30, 1858, photograph shows Grassy Island Lighthouse in the Detroit River near Mama Juda Island. Notice the large birdcage-style lantern room at the top of the tower. The first lighthouse was built in 1848 and rebuilt in 1858. The four lights on the island disappeared in the 1940s. (NARA.)

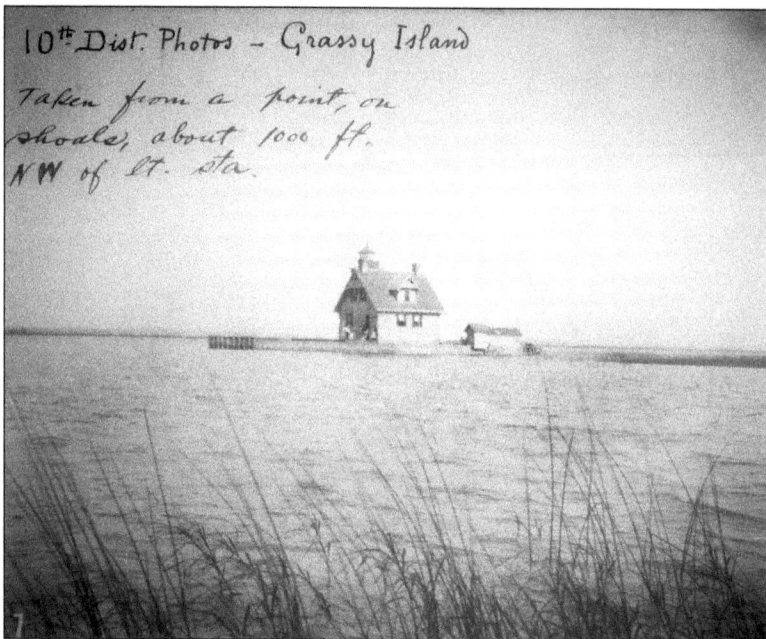

This is an early view of the Grassy Island South Channel Rear Range Lighthouse as it looked in 1896. (NARA.)

Notice that the steamboat to the left of the lighthouse also has masts for sails. Even steamboat builders were skeptical of their steam engines at the time and wanted a backup plan. Grassy Island South Channel Range Front Light is pictured here in 1896. (NARA.)

116

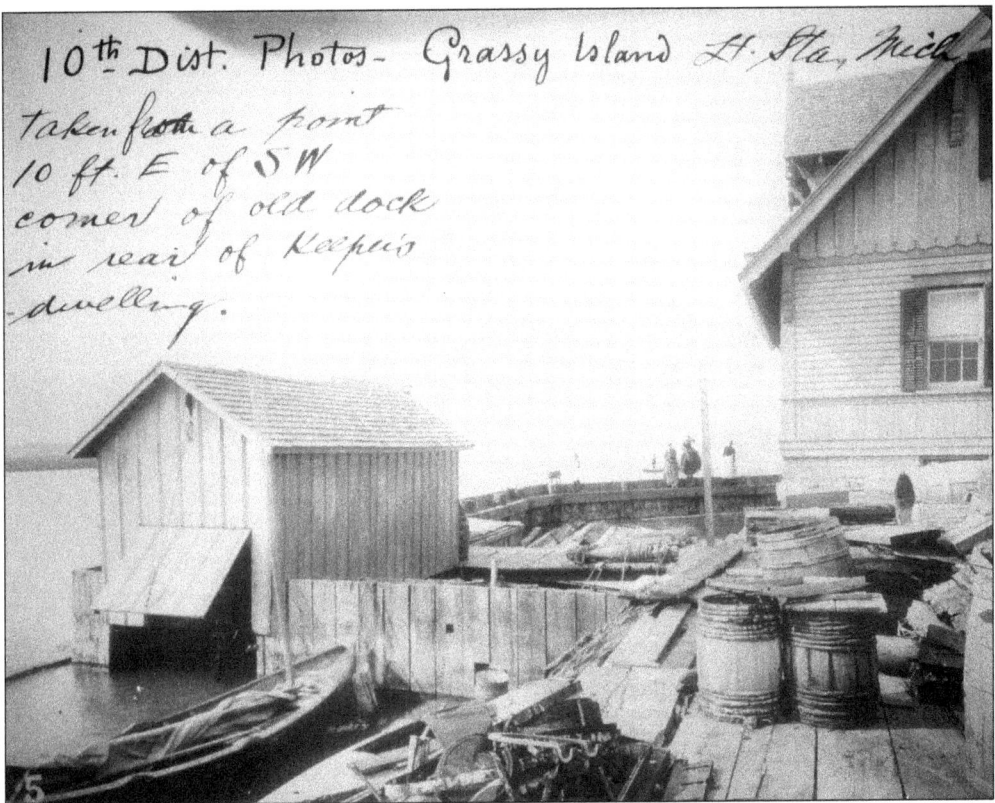

Pictured is the backyard of the Grassy Island South Channel Rear Range Lighthouse in 1896. The 10-year-old child seen walking the planks with a dog, to the left of the group of people, grew up watching sunrises and sunsets over the water and boats pass by the backyard. What a great place to grow up! (NARA.)

Grassy Island South Channel Rear Lighthouse became more attractive as it aged. Notice the fancy trim painted on the lighthouse and the oil container near the water. (USCG.)

The Grassy Island North Channel Rear Range Light is pictured to the left. The Grassy Island North Channel Front Range Light is pictured below. (USCG.)

The first lighthouse, built in 1838 at Gibraltar, 18 miles from Detroit, guided ships into the western channel of the Detroit River. It was rebuilt in 1873, pictured here. The last of nine keepers, Mary Vreeland replaced her husband in 1876. The lighthouse was discontinued in 1879, and the lantern room was moved to South Bass Island Lighthouse. It was sold in 1895 and demolished. (NARA.)

The first Monroe Lighthouse, built at Otter Creek, resembled the Barcelona Light on Lake Erie; no photographs are believed to exist. The lighthouse became obsolete when a new channel was dredged into Monroe Harbor, miles away. The second light, built in 1848–1849 and pictured here, has a birdcage-style lantern room. (GLHS.)

The third Monroe Lighthouse, pictured here, was built in 1884–1885. Nearby, a casino with a large dance floor and an amusement park were built, attracting excursion boats from Detroit and Toledo. In 1900, a Fourth Order Fresnel lens was installed, casting a light visible for 13 miles. When the popularity of the automobile increased, excursion boat travel decreased, and the casino closed. This beautiful lighthouse was deactivated in 1916 when an automated gaslight on a skeletal tower was installed on the pier. The light was sold in 1922 and destroyed. (Above, Walter P. Reuther Library, Wayne State University; below, AC.)

Ten

SHIPS THAT SELDOM SAIL

"The steep, oncoming wave towers over the bow of the lightship, its threatening size and force burning into my memory. I brace myself, grab onto a railing. In seconds the wall of water slams into the ship and it shutters. How much can the boat take, I wonder," reminisces one lightship sailor.

During a 100-mile-per-hour gale while anchored in the Strait of Juan de Fuca off of the Washington coast, Capt. Eric H. Lindman of lightship no. 113 *Swiftsure* wrote in December 1936: "The wind came shrieking and snarling out of the south. The sea writhed and steamed like a bowl of boiling milk. The air was full of tiny particles of water so thick we could barely see. The foghorn was blowing, but one could scarcely hear it. Objects broken loose . . . set up an unearthly clatter as they raced about . . . on the decks below." The lightship was anchored off the Washington coast when the hurricane hit.

During foggy conditions, other ships occasionally hit lightships. Around 1900, Capt. Dave Beggs of the 180-foot-long wooden steamer *Aztec* left Chicago for Montreal, Quebec, Canada, when dense fog developed. Up Lake Michigan, through Grays Reef Passage and the Straits of Mackinac, and then down Lake Huron his ship continued through thick mist. Clanging bells from other ships were heard, but no boats were ever seen. Captain Beggs's instinct told him to stop and anchor, that they were near the St. Clair River entrance, but no one heard the normal Lake Huron Lightship fog whistle. Unknown to them, the fog signal was not working. Eventually, the wind picked up, dispersed the fog, and brought a heart-stopping moment. Captain Beggs's intuition and remarkable seamanship were revealed: the boat's steering pole was tangled in the rigging of the Lake Huron Lightship only a few feet away.

Lake Huron Lightship LV 61 is pictured on November 20, 1914. It was placed north and west of Corsica Shoal on September 25, 1893, near the mouth of the St. Clair River, in 20 feet of water. It was moved to the Detroit Lighthouse Depot for repairs during the winter season. (NARA.)

Lake Huron Lightship LV 103 is the only museum of its kind on the Great Lakes. When in operation, a crew of 11 to 12 men worked nine months on the ship. They commented that it was great being on the vessel during fair weather, but when the fog rolled in it was a different story. The loud sound of the foghorn could last up to 36 hours, keeping everyone awake and causing the entire ship to vibrate. During free time, the men would read or play cards. The crew would work 21 days and then have 7 days off. (AC.)

Lake Huron Lightship LV 103, pictured as a museum at its berth near the Blue Water Bridge, was the third lightship at Corsica Shoals. Built in New York in 1920, it was brought to the Great Lakes and outfitted at the Detroit Lighthouse Depot, pictured below. It served as a relief ship at various stations in Lake Michigan, and the hull was painted a brilliant red with "HURON" in white lettering. In 1935, the vessel was transferred to Corsica Shoals in Lake Huron and anchored six miles north of the Blue Water Bridges and three miles east of the Michigan shoreline. It guided freighters into the channel leading to the St. Clair River. (AC.)

In 1970, upon retirement, the Coast Guard gave the lightship to the City of Grand Haven. Residents of Port Huron were extremely upset and went into action. Children wrote over 4,000 letters pleading for the lightship to remain; Jefferson schoolchildren alone assembled a petition 20 feet long. The Coast Guard relented, and on June 5, 1971, the lightship was given to the City of Port Huron. After numerous changes, the vessel opened to the public in 1990 as the only lightship museum on the Great Lakes. Various lighthouse tenders and lightships are seen docked at the Detroit Lighthouse Depot for repairs and outfitting. (Walter P. Reuther Library, Wayne State University.)

The 1902 St. Clair Lightship ILV 75, pictured here, was originally painted with "Grosse Pointe." Located in Lake St. Clair, it guided ships from the St. Clair River to the Detroit River. Its hull was painted bright red. The crew stated that in early spring and late fall, storms would bring snow, sleet, and frostbite. Chunks of ice in the water would scrape against the sides of the metal hull, and a man would observe that the ice did not puncture the boat. On-board duties involved cleaning lantern lamps, scrubbing, polishing, and fixing mechanical failures. Supplies were brought by the lighthouse tender *Marigold*. (NARA.)

In 1926, the St. Clair Lightship was the first remote-controlled lightship on the Great Lakes and the first vessel built to be completely automated. Its signaling systems were operated on shore eight miles away at Harsen's Island. When fog rolled in, the radio operator sent signals to start the foghorn. It was painted bright red with white lettering. The lightship operated for 27 years, and the Lake St. Clair crib lighthouse replaced it in 1939. (NARA.)

Poe Reef Lightship LV 99 was painted bright red with white lettering. Placed in upper Lake Huron over Poe Reef in July 1921, not far from shore, it was replaced by the Poe Reef Lighthouse in 1929. (NARA.)

Martin Reef Lightship LV 89 was stationed 12 miles north of Spectacle Reef and 25 miles northeast of the Straits of Mackinac prior to 1913. The reef posed a problem for ships traveling down the St. Mary's River and turning into the Straits of Mackinac. In 1913, the name was shortened to Martin. The Martin Reef Lighthouse was built, and the lightship was moved to the North Manitou Shoal in 1927. (NARA.)

LIGHTHOUSE MUSEUMS AND ORGANIZATIONS

CHEBOYGAN RIVER FRONT RANGE LIGHTHOUSE, GREAT LAKES LIGHTHOUSE KEEPERS ASSOCIATION. PO Box 219, Mackinaw City, MI, 44907-219. Phone: (231) 436-5580. Email: info@gllka.com. Website: www.gllka.com.

CHARITY ISLAND, CHARITY ISLAND TRANSPORT, INC. PO Box 171, Au Gres, MI, 48703. Contact: www.charityisland.net/contact.html. Website: www.charity island.net

DETOUR REEF LIGHT, DETOUR REEF LIGHT PRESERVATION SOCIETY. PO Box 307, Drummond Island, MI, 49726. Phone: (906) 493-6609. Email: drips@drips.com. Website: www.drips.com.

FORT GRATIOT LIGHT, PORT HURON MUSEUM. 1115 Sixth Street, Port Huron, MI, 48060. Phone: (810) 982-0891. Website: www.phmuseum.org.

FORTY MILE POINT LIGHT, 40 MILE POINT LIGHTHOUSE SOCIETY. PO Box 205, Rogers City, MI, 49779. Website: www.40milepointlighthouse.org.

GREAT LAKES LIGHTHOUSE KEEPERS ASSOCIATION. PO Box 219, Mackinaw City, MI, 49701-219. Phone: (231) 436-5580. Email: info@gllka.com. Website: www.gllka.com.

GREAT LAKES HISTORICAL SOCIETY AND INLAND SEAS MARITIME MUSEUM now NATIONAL GREAT LAKES MUSEUM. Moving in 2013 to 1701 Front Street, Toledo, OH, 43605. Phone: (440) 967-3467 and (800) 893-1485. Website: www.inlandseas.org.

GROSSE POINT LIGHTHOUSE, GROSSE POINT LIGHTHOUSE MUSEUM. 2601 Sheridan Road.

HARBOR BEACH LIGHTHOUSE, HARBOR BEACH LIGHTHOUSE AND BREAKWALL PRESERVATION SOCIETY. 926 Lakeview Drive, Harbor Beach, MI, 48441.

HURON LIGHTSHIP LV103, PORT HURON MUSEUM. 1115 Sixth Street, Port Huron, MI, 48060. Phone: (810) 982-0891. Email: lightship@phmuseum.org. Website: www.phmuseum.org.

MIDDLE ISLAND LIGHTHOUSE, MIDDLE ISLAND BED AND BREAKFAST. 5671 Rockport Road, Alpena, MI, 49707. Phone: (989) 356-1385.

POINTE AUX BARQUES LIGHTHOUSE, POINTE AUX BARQUES LIGHTHOUSE SOCIETY. PO Box 97, Port Hope, MI, 48468-9759. Phone: (989) 428-2010. Email: info@pointeauxbarqueslighthouse.org Website: www.pointeauxbarqueslighthouse.org.

PORT AUSTIN REEF, PORT AUSTIN REEF LIGHT ASSOCIATION. PO Box 546, Port Austin, MI, 48467.

PRESQUE ISLE LIGHTHOUSE, NEW PRESQUE ISLE LIGHTHOUSE PARK AND MUSEUM. 4500 East Grand Lake Road, Presque Isle, MI, 49777. Phone: (989) 595-5419.

SAGINAW RIVER REAR RANGE LIGHTHOUSE, SAGINAW RIVER MARINE HISTORICAL SOCIETY. Department SB, PO Box 2051, Bay City, MI, 48707-2051. Phone: (989) 686-1895. Website: www.saginawriver.com.

STURGEON POINT LIGHTHOUSE, ALCONA HISTORICAL SOCIETY. PO Box 174, Harrisville, MI, 48740. Phone: (989) 724-5107. Contact: www.theenchantedforest.com/AlconaHistoricalSociety.

TAWAS LIGHTHOUSE, TAWAS POINT STATE PARK. 686 Tawas Beach Road, East Tawas, MI, 48730. Phone: (989) 362-5041 or (989) 362-5658.

THUNDER BAY LIGHTHOUSE, THUNDER BAY ISLAND LIGHTHOUSE PRESERVATION SOCIETY. PO Box 212, Alpena, MI, 49707. Email: info@thunderbayislandsociety.org. Website: www.thungerbayislandsociety.org.

BIBLIOGRAPHY

Adamson, Hans Christian, *Keepers of the Lights*. New York: Greenberg, 1955.

Bak, Richard. *Detroit: A Postcard History*. Charleston, SC: Arcadia Publishing, 1998.

Boyer, Dwight. *Strange Adventures of the Great Lakes*. Cleveland, OH: Freshwater Press, 1974.

Chicago Record-Herald, 1913.

Cleveland Plain Dealer, 1924.

Detroit Free Press, 1913.

Duluth Herald, 1913.

Fornes, Mike. *Mackinac Bridge: A 50-Year Chronicle, 1957–2007*. Mackinaw City, MI: Cheboygan Tribune Printing Co., 2007.

Gaffney, T.J. *Port Huron, 1880–1960*. Charleston, SC: Arcadia Publishing, 2006.

Gervais, Marty. *The Rumrunners: A Prohibition Scrapbook*. Emeryville, ON, Canada: self-published, 1980–2009.

Grosse Ile Historical Society. *Grosse Ile*. Charleston, SC: Arcadia Publishing, 2007.

Harrison, Timothy E. *Ghost Lights of Lake Erie*. East Machias, ME: Foghorn Publishing, 2010.

———. *Ghost Lights of Michigan*. Foghorn Publishing, 2009.

Hill, Jeff. *Defining Moments: Prohibition*. Detroit: Omnigraphics Inc., 2004.

Kadar, Wayne Louis. *Great Lakes Passenger Ship Disasters*. Quinn, MI: Avery Color Studios Inc., 2005

Mason, Philip P. *Rumrunning and the Roaring Twenties*. Detroit: Wayne State University Press, 1995.

North, Tom. *Mackinac Island*. Charleston, SC: Arcadia Publishing, 2011.

Pepper, Terry. *Lighting the Straits of Mackinac*. Mackinaw, MI: The Great Lakes Lighthouse Keepers Association, 2000.

Rodriguez, Michael and Thomas Featherstone. *Detroit's Belle Isle–Island Park Gem*. Charleston, SC: Arcadia Publishing, 2003.

Socia, Madeleine and Suzy Berschback. *Grosse Pointe: 1880–1930*. Charleston, SC: Arcadia Publishing, 2001.

Stonehouse, Frederick. *Haunted Lake Huron*. Duluth, MN: Lake Superior Port Cities, 2007.

Toledo Blade, 1913.

Tongue, Stephen D. *Lanterns & Lifeboats*. Alpena, MI: Sarge Publishing, 2004.

Wright, Larry and Patricia Wright. *Great Lakes Lighthouse Encyclopedia*. Erin, ON, Canada: Boston Mills Press, 2006.

———. *Lightships of the Great Lakes*. Self-published, 2011.

Visit us at
arcadiapublishing.com